# FINDING THE QUIET

# PAUL WILSON

# FINDING THE

# QUIET

Four simple steps to peace
and contentment—without
spending the rest of your life
on a mountaintop

JEREMY P. TARCHER/PENGUIN

a member of Penguin Group (USA) Inc.

New York

JEREMY P. TARCHER/PENGUIN
Published by the Penguin Group
Penguin Group (USA) Inc., 375 Hudson Street, New York,
New York 10014, USA • Penguin Group (Canada), 90 Eglinton Avenue East, Suite 700, Toronto,
Ontario M4P 2Y3, Canada (a division of Pearson Canada Inc.) • Penguin Books Ltd, 80 Strand, London
WC2R 0RL, England • Penguin Ireland, 25 St Stephen's Green, Dublin 2, Ireland (a division of Penguin
Books Ltd) • Penguin Group (Australia), 250 Camberwell Road, Camberwell, Victoria 3124, Australia
(a division of Pearson Australia Group Pty Ltd) • Penguin Books India Pvt Ltd, 11 Community Centre,
Panchsheel Park, New Delhi–110 017, India • Penguin Group (NZ), 67 Apollo Drive, Rosedale, North
Shore 0632, New Zealand (a division of Pearson New Zealand Ltd) • Penguin Books (South Africa) (Pty) Ltd,
24 Sturdee Avenue, Rosebank, Johannesburg 2196, South Africa

Penguin Books Ltd, Registered Offices: 80 Strand, London WC2R 0RL, England

Originally published in Australia as *The Quiet* by Pan Macmillan Australia Pty Ltd 2006
First published in the United States by Jeremy P. Tarcher/Penguin 2009
Text copyright © by The Calm Centre Pty Ltd 2006
Illustrations copyright © 2006 by Wendy Blume

Most Tarcher/Penguin books are available at special quantity discounts for bulk purchase
for sales promotions, premiums, fund-raising, and educational needs. Special books or book
excerpts also can be created to fit specific needs. For details, write Penguin Group (USA) Inc.
Special Markets, 375 Hudson Street, New York, NY 10014.

Library of Congress Cataloging-in-Publication Data

Wilson, Paul, date.
Finding the quiet: four simple steps to peace and contentment—without spending
the rest of your life on a mountaintop / Paul Wilson.
p.      cm.
ISBN 978-1-58542-705-5
1. Peace of mind.   2. Contentment.   3. Quietude.   I. Title.
BF637.P3W55      2009                    2009012754
158.1'2—dc22

Printed in the United States of America
1   3   5   7   9   10   8   6   4   2

# FINDING THE QUIET

## BOOK A

# CONTENTS

# SOMETHING ELSE

A fter a decade of touring, writing, and speaking as "the Guru of Calm," it was time to step out of the limelight. What I had in mind was a few years at home, combined with some small-scale teaching and some large-scale surfing.

This would have worked well had I not been invited to India in 2002. You'd think a small conference of unrelated writers, teachers, and assorted others would be fairly harmless. Exactly what I thought. I was totally unprepared for the following exchange.

"Guruji wants to know what you are writing these days, Mr. Wilson." I said I was taking it easy. A bit of teaching, and a lot more surfing.

Silence.

Not wishing to appear too underoccupied compared with the industrious people who had invited me, I quickly added that I was conducting the occasional meditation retreat, where I taught a streamlined approach to meditation.

More silence.

In the politest possible way it was suggested that, in light of my talents and reputation, perhaps my work wasn't finished yet. Later that evening it was further suggested that my future work might not be surfing, but to "spread joy and remove sorrow."

Spreading joy didn't seem like a bad sort of role to take on, although removing sorrow (or removing *suffering*, as it was later retranslated) wasn't something I'd had much experience in.

I didn't give much thought to either of these messages until the flight home. I wondered if there might be some sort of link between them and another comment that had been made on that visit.

In Mumbai, a journalist wondered why the people of that city were buying my books. I'd wondered the same thing myself. With so many indigenous gurus and meditation schools for them to choose from, surely my offerings would be seen as more or less of the same.

"It's the *noise*," she suggested. "When you live in a city of 15 million people that's teeming with life 24 hours a day, there is very little relief from the noise. Your books offer a way to escape it."

Providing relief from noise? I hadn't thought of noise that way before. We take for granted the racket we live with—not only physical noise, but emotional and intellectual "noise" as well. It's become so dense and unremitting that when a gap does occasionally appear, it suggests that something's wrong. There's a *space*—but what does that mean? Does "space" equal "quiet"? Or does it mean that something is missing? There are so few gaps or spaces to be found that it's almost as if we've become detuned to their restorative power. We've become detuned to the subtlety and beauty of silence. Detuned to the joy of just being.

Spreading joy, removing sorrow, and providing relief from noise . . . I had plenty to think about on that flight back home.

Now that you're thinking about it as well, you can probably see the appeal of having more space in your life. And more quiet. And more joy and peace. Perhaps that's why you've picked up this book in the first place.

When you were in your teens, you would never have guessed it could turn out like this. Then you were looking forward to all the freedom you'd have when you grew up. Not to mention the joy and happiness.

What happened?

Today, instead of doing the things you'd always wanted to, your day's taken up by things that others want you to do, or you have to do, or you think you have to do. Instead of being the one who calls the shots, you're the one being dictated to by bosses, mortgages, school lunches, politicians, and even terrorists on the other side of the world. Instead of being in charge of your own time, time is in charge of you. As for a light at the end of the tunnel, you can't even see the tunnel.

When you were in your teens you probably thought that the material side of life would provide the satisfaction you were looking for. Back then you had no doubt that the more you acquired, the happier you'd be: more possessions, more friends, more adventures, more accomplishments. Who'd have thought you would arrive at the conclusion that it was going to take *less* for you to feel happy? Less work, less clutter, less complication, less responsibility. More or less—both were illusions, and neither was the key.

So what's it going to take? What makes life worthwhile? What brings happiness and satisfaction?

Like all of us, you've already discovered how fleeting happiness is. It ebbs and flows according to whatever happens on the day. You fall in love, and everything is light and exciting. A sharp exchange with your partner and you're angry and depressed. Have a new baby, and the world is infused with purpose and hope. A bad news day in the media and you're heavy with despair. Take a new job, win a prize, get out on the right side of the bed, and you find it hard to remember ever feeling down. But you know it's coming. Even at the peak of·your delight, something inside warns that it can't last. And it can't.

There must be something else.

Look around and you'll see that certain people seem to have discovered this "something else." On the surface they're not all that different from you and me: they live everyday lives, work just as hard, have just as many pressures and responsibilities, and face the same ups and downs as we all do. But then there's that something else. They seem to have space in their lives. They seem happy and fulfilled. They exude an unmistakable air of peace and equanimity. They give you the impression that whatever is going on is okay and in order—as if it has some deeper meaning, but may be fun nevertheless. Sometimes there's even a childlike sense of adventure that goes with it all.

What do they know that most of the world doesn't? Why do they always seem so content, when almost everyone you know is under some sort of pressure? How do they avoid the fears and insecurities that seem to mark life for the rest of us? Why are they the only ones not complaining about long work hours, or lack of values, or the pace of modern life? What is the something else that they've found, but we're still looking for?

In so many instances, it's meditation.

Meditation is one of the few sustainable ways of ensuring peace and happiness in life. It is a methodical way of relieving disquiet and mental suffering. It is a reliable way of adding space to your day and your environment. And it is the only predictable way of realizing direct spiritual fulfillment and enlightenment.

There are hundreds of different roads to peace, happiness, and enlightenment. Thousands. Ancient and contemporary. Ranging from traditions that date back thousands of years to lifestyle movements that were thought up a few days ago.

If you were to choose one of these paths, do you have the commitment to see it through? With so much on your plate already, you might wonder how you could possibly accommodate one more thing.

Then again, you might wonder whether it's too early to start yet. It's tempting to leave it until you're older and have fewer things on your mind. Maybe you think it's too late to start. Maybe you believe you are too much of this world—too focused on your job, home, relationships, or ambitions—to even consider things that sound more spiritual in nature.

Maybe you did what hundreds of thousands of others have done, and learned to meditate, attended a retreat or two, then let it lapse, or didn't quite get it, or didn't have the patience for the packaging that came with it.

Even assuming you have the heart for the journey, it's easy to become confused by all the possible routes. Narrowing it down to any particular one is a huge task. How can you be sure the choice you make today will be the appropriate one in 20 or 30 years' time, or when you're preparing to depart this world? It's not like the old days when everyone was certain of where they were headed, of what was required to get there, and of what they could expect when they arrived. Today we're far too sophisticated for such beliefs. We know too much. And, ironically, we really do believe this at exactly the same time as we admit we know nothing at all.

Meditation is the way through this maze.

Traditional meditation approaches can be every bit as demanding and confusing as the many spiritual choices. The meditation approach described in this book may not be as extensive as some of the traditions, but you will be able to understand it. You won't have to immerse yourself in endless study, and, regardless of the stage or complexity of your life, you'll find it much easier to make it part of your day.

For the moment, let's call it **the Quiet approach**.

Once you get the hang of it, the Quiet approach will become the cornerstone of your day. Not just because it brings a bit of peace and stability to your life, but because you find it profoundly fulfilling. You start noticing changes in yourself, such as a new sense of clarity emerging. Before your very eyes, things start falling into place.

But the main reason it becomes the cornerstone of your day is that it doesn't *expect* you to change. The Quiet approach takes into account that you're a contemporary person leading a conventional life. It offers you a range of choices, and doesn't lock you into any one in particular. If you think one way today but come across something more appealing tomorrow, no worries—you don't have to start again. You're on the right path.

Now, let me bring this into sharper focus for you.

*Finding the Quiet* is going to show you how setting aside a few moments each day—as little as 13 minutes—can put you on the path to achieving all those benefits outlined above. Yes, the lot: peace, happiness, contentment, clarity, and purpose. And yes, all in just 13 minutes. If you're currently practicing some sort of meditation, you may want to extend this period a bit.

As long as you can turn this page with an open mind, and be prepared to enjoy the stages ahead as you encounter them, you'll immediately start to develop a skill that has the potential to transform your life in the most extraordinary way.

And you can do this to whatever extent you believe appropriate or feel comfortable with.

With very little effort, you'll discover what it takes to be happier, more loving, more contented. You'll feel healthier and more settled than you have for ages. You'll find more *space* in your life. You'll find yourself becoming spiritually connected and aware. You will start to develop deeper insights to your own nature and the world around you. There is no limit to this process.

By the time my plane touched down in Sydney, I was planning this book. There *was* a foolproof way I could bring joy to people's lives. Surprisingly simple, too. And this same way could remove tension, anxiety, fear, suffering, and many of the other things you might lump under the heading of "sorrow."

All it would take was for me to point out a unique state or realization known as **the Quiet**. And to explain the four brief steps that would lead you there. (These steps make up **the Quiet practices** described in this book.)

This is why the "spreading joy" part is going to be a piece of cake. It occurs in two distinct ways. Initially through the Quiet practices themselves; then through the results they produce.

The practices you're going to read about are pleasing in themselves, in the sense that they lead to a state that is both relaxed and enjoyable. Some people describe this state in grander terms, but I think such descriptions are better left till later.

The results are also for further down the track. At the very minimum, following the Quiet practices will make you feel better and lead to a happier, more harmonious state of mind. Taken much further, they can lead to an ongoing state that may be described as blissful or ecstatic.

This brings us to the "removing sorrow" part.

If we look at it from a personal point of view rather than a global one, most suffering comes from comparatively trivial things. Instead of being the result of war and famine, it's more likely to be the culmination of long work hours or relationship tensions. Or a response to abstract threats like global warming, terrorism, bird flu, recession, or tsunami; or to even less substantial things, such as those mentioned in a recent research group I conducted. The following are all direct quotes:

- *"I'm starting to despair about all the violence and nihilism in the world right now. It's really depressing."*
- *"By most people's standards, I'm leading a comfortable life. But something's missing. I never feel settled."*
- *"All I do is work."*
- *"It's all too fast. I need to slow down, to find some peace of mind."*
- *"I've always wanted to learn meditation, but who can find the time?"*
- *"On one hand we've got all this pressure to consume more, to produce more. But on the other, I want life to be simpler, and to do less."*

The Quiet practices work wonders in helping you escape the tension and unsettledness of the modern world. With very little effort, they lead to peace of mind, clarity of thought, and emotional stability as well as physical well-being.

But all that is only the first step.

When I wrote *The Calm Technique* in the 1980s, my focus was on benefits such as these. That book's premise was that meditation could be a vital supplement to a hectic modern lifestyle—a competitive edge, if you like—and that you could derive all the here-and-now benefits without getting too involved in the spiritual side.

*Finding the Quiet* still encompasses the here and now, but provides the tools for enriching your spiritual life as well, in whichever way appeals to you. This is a huge story. One that builds on thousands of years of knowledge and practice. One that's built on 40 years of my own meditation experience, and 20 years of research.

But unlike many of the traditional methods, this one is immediate and accessible to anyone living in our world now.

Having made the comparison with the traditional methods, you might wonder about the background to the Quiet approach. Are its origins in Buddhism, Yoga, Transcendental Meditation, Christianity, or something else? The answer is yes. And no.

My training and research came from a variety of traditional schools but I was always a freelancer at heart. That way, I've been able to experiment with a wide variety of practices—and shamelessly take the best parts from each. Later I'll explain how my methods came into being, and how they relate to the traditions.

It's not uncommon in the traditional schools for a large percentage of what's taught to be profound, with the remainder being a combination of myth and window dressing. This applies not just to the spiritually oriented disciplines like meditation, but to those associated with the arts, medicine, and martial arts as well. With the help of some great teachers, several generations of meditators, psychological researchers, and access to evaluative technology such as the electroencephalogram (EEG), I've been able to identify an underlying methodology that encompasses all major meditation styles and approaches, and dispense with most of the distracting stuff. The result is a demystified set of practices, designed for a contemporary, short-attention-span world.

The four steps of the Quiet approach produce all the short- to medium-term benefits of traditional meditation, but in an easier and more understandable way. Even though the major benefits may take more time, the Quiet approach enables you to go the whole way yourself—if that is what you choose—without intensive training and without committing to any particular spiritual path.

The ultimate destination is a place I call **the Quiet**. As it's a state of mind as much as anything else, it will accommodate all spiritual paths. Knowing this from the beginning means you can let go of your expectations and just give in to what's happening as it happens. Start with a few physical steps that anyone can master and apply, intensify it with a few tweaks of understanding and consciousness, and you're on the way.

This is what Book A of *Finding the Quiet* is all about. It relates to mastering the method, while Book B relates to where it can take you. The first book is like learning to ride a surfboard; the second is like taking on the Banzai Pipeline.

Next, there's a built-in pace to what's ahead, if not a lazy pace, then certainly a leisurely one. Think of it as a stroll through some relaxing concepts, some of which are vigorous and new, while others have been lazing around for eons. There's no hurry. No deadlines. So just relax and enjoy the process of discovery. Go as far as you feel comfortable, then put the book aside until you're ready to go further. (Personally, I find it helps to take regular breaks every now and then to let it all soak in.)

To remind you of this, you'll come across pauses at strategic places throughout the text. These aren't intended to be exercises so much as places of consolidation—little time-outs, or mini-meditations, if you like. You'll recognize them by this symbol:

Then, there's the path. When you get to Book B, you'll discover there are several to consider. However, there's no pressure to choose any.

Which brings us, finally, to the duration. The Quiet approach is a lifetime project. Depending on your point of view, perhaps more than a lifetime project. The key is to forget about timing, forget about results, forget about the benefits, and just enjoy whatever unfolds. You succeed when you enjoy the process.

There's also the possibility that you'll find all you need tomorrow. Should this happen, pass the book to someone who needs it more. That's how it's meant to work. On the other hand, if it takes you a year to get to the part that changes your life, that's also how it's meant to work. You have all the time in the world.

You also have all the space you need. Whether "space" equals "peace" equals "the Quiet" is for you to discover in the pages ahead. But first you have to overcome the way a busy, demanding lifestyle detunes you to the power of space and silence.

Fortunately, there is not a single thing you have to do to overcome this. Because it's only when you *cease* doing certain things that it occurs. It's only when you can let go of your expectations and be open to whatever comes along. When you let go of the need to manage and control—so you can just enjoy whatever eventuates. When you let go of your need to analyze and dissect—so you can appreciate whatever arises in the instant that it happens. When you let go of thinking about what you're experiencing—so that you can just experience it for what it is.

Let go and enjoy the ride.

# THE UNDERLYING QUIET

When things are really still, you may hear it. It's the space between sounds, between thoughts, between experiences.

It's a precious, but elusive, kind of quiet. When—if—you hear it, you don't think of an absence of sound. Quite the opposite. It's more the presence of something rather than the absence. The presence of peace and tranquility. The presence of a disposition that is untroubled by stress and emotion. Or of a period free from disturbance of any kind. The presence of calm.

As well as bringing peace, it also brings meaning. It adds richness to relationships, enhances communication, deepens your spiritual understanding and fulfillment.

You're still thinking of sound, aren't you? Let's bring another sense into play. What does it *feel* like?

*Shhh*. Pause for a moment. Listen to your feelings . . .

When I suggest there's a quiet place inside you—deep inside you—you start to move away from this relationship with sound. You start to *feel* something. Perhaps a subtle impression that grows as you read this. Your subconscious whispers that here's a place where you will feel safe and secure. Where the outside world can't touch you. Where you find peace. You feel that all you need to do is pause for a moment . . . and allow the external static to fade . . . and just relax into that stillness at the core of your being.

You feel, you sense, you know that being in this place now is not an "escape from," it's a "coming to." It's familiar. There's no need to do, think, or understand here. Everything makes sense.

When you have a harmonious relationship with the world around you, when you gently turn your attention inward, when your breathing slows and your thoughts settle . . . this is the place you come to.

This is **the Quiet**.

You know how to find peace and quiet when you're on the mountaintop, in the forest, on the secluded beach, at the retreat center, or in the ancient temple. It's there for the taking. But how do you find it in the thick of a noisy, nonstop modern world? How do you find it when you're battling to make a living, raise the children, and deal with illness? How do you summon it for those moments when you're furthest away, when you need it the most?

It's a rare gift to be able to go through life feeling grounded in a peaceful, meaningful place. People who have this gift enjoy a sense of inner calm that is almost meditative in nature. Whatever they do, whomever they're with, it's never far from the surface. They can come back to it at any time. It's their shortcut to the Quiet.

For some, it becomes a foundation for their spiritual explorations and practices. For others, it means they can throw themselves into the deep end of life, knowing that there's an inner strength and order they can call on if they need it. No matter what is going on around them, no matter their responsibilities, deadlines, or pressures.

Some devote a lifetime to finding it, through years of rigorous, often uncomfortable training and study designed to liberate themselves from the ego as well as the noise and distractions of the material world. Others find it with the greatest of ease, sometimes with only the most subtle shift of understanding. And, of course, billions never find it at all.

I discovered the Quiet during childhood. While the passage of time and 40-odd years of meditation practice have broadened my understanding of what it is, this disovery has stayed with me all along. It's with me as I write this.

If things get challenging, I can tap into it. A deep sense of peace and certainty comes flooding back, no matter what's going on around me. It works in a traffic snarl in Rome, on a stage in London, in a noisy restaurant in Madrid, on a crowded train in India (well, almost). A fleeting recall is all it takes.

Maybe you can see the appeal of this. At the very least, it would be an effective way of taking your mind off the pressures and tensions of the everyday. But more than that, the Quiet can take you beyond worries, regrets, fears, and insecurities. Beyond all of life's hassles and the things you have to do or should have done. It can take you right to the underlying stillness of life, the spiritual essence of all there is, the heart of peace and happiness.

Here you discover how good it is to have time and space for everything. For the more elevating things. To venture beyond your current state of health or happiness, beyond your roles and masks. To be able to focus on peace and beauty. To wonder about, and come into contact with, infinity.

# Where it arises

You will be able to access the Quiet by using the skills and understanding you'll take from this book.

It's possible to access it in other ways, though. It can be built on the most modest of realizations or recollections—say, from a physical place or experience. It can be stimulated emotionally: by a painting, a line of poetry, the recollection of a smile or touch, an uplifting story, the feeling you get when you think of your mother.

Sometimes it arises from unlikely places. On a lecture tour I was approached by a woman who had recently recovered from a long bout of illness. Her version of the Quiet had been the foundation of her recovery. For such an accomplishment, you might've thought it would be based on something grand or inspiring, but it came from an innocuous line in my talk on mental states. I remember the words: "You might remember those blissful twilight moments of an evening, when your eyelids are heavy, your thoughts have come to rest. Those peaceful, timeless moments just as you feel yourself drifting off . . ." Why that particular sentiment was so meaningful to her is anybody's guess, but she'd turned it into something more powerful than it was intended to be.

If you are open to the underlying peacefulness of an event, there's no limit to the places the Quiet can come from.

You no longer hear the orchestra, and you have no awareness of the melody; all you can feel is the swell of your heart and the tears in your eyes . . . As far as the eyes can see, there are snow-topped mountains, bottomless chasms and valleys, and proof that there is some greater force at play in the world . . . Nothing needs to be said or analyzed because there is so much love in your life. You feel it. You give it. It is all around you . . .

Maybe it relates to a specific mental state. An altered state of consciousness such as deep meditation, or a spiritual insight, or any number of other so-called peak experiences.

You've probably had a peak experience at some time during your life. It can occur of its own accord or can be induced by drugs, but mostly it's stimulated by unexpected events.

A peak experience takes you out of yourself, and produces intense feelings of well-being and happiness. Possibly even ecstasy. For a moment, everything seems to fall into place. You have a sense of being a part of something much bigger. Often it is accompanied by brief insights into big questions such as the meaning of life—but these are fleeting and can't be satisfactorily described or explained. Above all, though, a peak experience is inspiring, positive, and unforgettable.

From a worldly point of view you might experience it as the result of an artistic performance or winning a sporting event. It could be the result of deep insight, love at first sight, profound rapport with another, great natural beauty, heroism, a medical recovery, or the feeling that you're in the presence of something sacred.

Maybe you could describe it as being spiritual in nature, but it needn't be religious or mystical.

If you can recall having had an experience such as this, turn your mind to it now, and you'll find those original feelings return. They might not be as intense or as complex as the first time, but you'll still experience them.

*There was a time in your past when everything fell into place. You probably felt deeply relaxed and at peace.*

*It may have been the place that made you feel this*
*way—a mountaintop, a secluded island, a Japanese garden,*
*a rain forest, a gently flowing stream, the seaside, a church,*
*a park, a quiet corner of your house.*

*It may have been the company—a lover, a parent, a*
*child in your arms. It may have been a line of poetry. It may*
*have been an inspired performance, or an act of heroism or*
*survival.*

*Maybe it's only in your imagination—a place you'd*
*love to visit, or an experience you'd love to have. The place*
*or the event doesn't really matter. All that's important is the*
*feeling that it brings to mind.*

*Spend a few moments in that recollection. Remember*
*how peaceful or inspiring it felt. Take your time and enjoy it.*

Even at that most superficial level, you would have reexperienced
some of the original feeling. The experiment was designed to appeal
to a rather limited level of consciousness, one that involves your
mind or thoughts.

The next experiment will take you a little deeper.

This time, your experience will involve your body as well as your
mind.

*Referring back to your experience in the previous exercise …*

*Close your eyes and slowly begin to imagine where you*
*first had this experience.*

*What does it look like? The colors, the textures, the*
*surfaces, the time of day. What are your surroundings?*

*What are you wearing? What is your posture? What is the expression on your face?*

*Don't try to force the image. Let it come if it's going to; otherwise just pretend that you can see it.*

*Then turn your attention to what you can hear. The applause, the music, the birds, the children's voices. Can you hear your own breathing? Does it sound different—slower, more relaxed—than usual?*

*Now turn your attention to what you can taste or smell. The taste of salt on your lips. The smell of roses or perfume.*

*And when you can imagine yourself actually being there—seeing your surroundings through your own eyes, hearing the sounds, tasting the tastes, smelling the scents— turn your attention to what you feel. The tingle down your spine as the curtain rises. The warmth of the sun on your face, the soft snow beneath your feet, the breeze against your back, the texture of the chair, the touch of a loved one.*

*Hold that feeling.*


Did you find that this was more real and intense than before? That's because you were experiencing it with all of your physical being, not just your mind. Another of the important discoveries ahead is that the integration of mind and body—where you rely less on analytical thinking and more on what you are sensing—will bring you closer to the Quiet.

Now, if I could ask you to let go of memories and fantasies for a while, and forget what you're feeling or experiencing, I'd like to take you to the place where I discovered the Quiet.

# Beyond the body-mind

This is not a story about a place. It is set in the late 1950s, but it's not about an age. Nor is it about a particular event, although I was definitely there.

It's about a realization.

This is an unusually remote part of the world. A dusty little corner of the Australian outback. The first impression you get here is of space. Vastness.

Depending on the time of year, another impression might be of heat; summer temperatures of 122 degrees Fahrenheit are common. It's dry, too, which is what you'd expect in the driest permanently inhabited part of this planet.

The mention of "inhabited" might raise your expectations. But look around . . . there are places here where you can turn from horizon to horizon without seeing a single feature. Not a hill, nor a rocky outcrop, nor a drift of wildflowers. Sometimes not even a tree. Just horizon. Endless red soil and blue sky, intersected by a dirt road that heads off to someplace unimaginable, without so much as a curve or intersection to break the monotony.

So you turn your attention to what you can hear. Nothing stands out? That's because it's what you *don't* hear that I'm trying to draw your attention to.

Listen again.

Stop listening for individual sounds—listen for what's behind the sounds. Not ambient noise, because there's no ambient noise out here most of the time. If you hear a sound, what's the background to that sound?

You're aware of it, aren't you? And yet there's nothing to be aware of—there's nothing to be heard!

Breathing  
Noises  
Ambient  
Underlying

It takes a big shift of awareness to become aware of what's not there, but once it happens your perception is never the same again. You realize the characteristic that defines this place is not remoteness, heat, or dryness—it's space. Not vastness, but gaping, empty space. Not what is here, but what is not. Not what you can determine by your senses, but what you determine without them. Not what you can reason, but what you intuit. Not what is manifest, but what is not manifest.

This shift of awareness can't take place until you abandon the influence of the body–mind. Abandon trying to analyze. Abandon the senses. In this case, give up trying to hear. Once you do that, you'll still hear individual sounds, but they will exist in relief; it's what sits beneath them that is in your awareness. This is more than just the spaces between individual noises; it's a complete absence of sound.

This is what we refer to as **the underlying quiet**. If you can imagine it, you're not far from the Quiet.

A change of consciousness is required for this. You get a hint of what this is like in the outback. One moment you're aware of isolated sounds and noises, the next moment your attention has gone past them, past the ambient whisper of the breeze, to the background *space* in which they arise. This is the reverse of your experience in the material world, where you're aware of sounds but never the space in which they arise; where you're aware of the object in space, but never the space itself.

Empty space. The mind struggles to characterize this. Space has no characteristics: it is dimensionless, featureless, timeless. Like an acoustic black hole. Immeasurable; impenetrable; unfathomable. And, even harder to imagine at this moment, it's not "out there" at all—you are in the center of it.

If I could instantly transport you to the outback now—from your familiar world of noise and communication overload, to this space in which individual sounds arise—you'd find the comparison breathtaking. There are other places where you might have a similar experience: a mountaintop, the Arctic plains, ballooning, gliding, under water, ocean sailing, meditation. But I first experienced it in the outback.

My favorite spot was a small clump of mulga trees in the middle of nowhere. They offered the only shade for miles. From the age of nine or so, I used to ride there most days and just sit. I can't remember if I was waiting for something to happen or just waiting for the heat to subside, but it seems I spent a large proportion of my boyhood there. Thinking up stories, planning my drawings, alone with my thoughts and observations.

On hearing this, some people tut-tut and say what a shame it is that a child has to lead such a lonely life. They don't understand that solitude is not loneliness. It's like open space. Faced with extended periods of this, you reach the point when you have to decide whether to look for distraction or go further into the solitude and see where it leads.

Going further into the solitude was the lesson of my life. Instead of impatience, there is tranquility. Instead of boredom, wonder. If you turn your thoughts to it now, you may sense this. No obligations or responsibilities. No awareness of the passage of time. No thoughts of the past. Fascinated by stillness. Unaware of the absence of stimuli.

Where, in your own immature way, you're sucked into speculations on the nature of now, eternity, and the limitlessness of imagination. Then you go beyond imagination.

You sense that you're part of something greater. There's no other possibility when your universe is defined by space. Even in the most obvious sense, it's inescapable. Hinted at by unimaginably broad daytime skies and horizons. Confirmed by nighttime skies that seem to expand even more. Stars that don't twinkle, but *beam* at you. So startlingly close and brilliant, they make you more a part of the universe than an inhabitant of Earth. The infinite, the Quiet, almost within the grasp of your imagination . . .

*Then it's gone.*

That was the confusing part—you can't even imagine it. You can be aware of it in the moment it occurs, but if you look back and wonder, *What was that?*, it's like it was never there. If you try to anticipate it, it won't return. You can only be aware of it as it happens.

Clearly this has something to do with being present. But there's more to it than that. Maybe it's the space that does it. Not the space between things, but the space that they appear in. Maybe the space in which stars arise is the same space in which sounds arise. Maybe this is the connection between all the different parts of life, and you can only be aware of it in the most fleeting instant. It's so simple that even a child is too sophisticated to get it. So obvious that it's impossible to see.

A shift in my perception began then. I can't remember whether it was sudden or took years, but I still rely on it. More than an awareness of the present, it's an awareness of space, the all-encompassing ground from which phenomena arise. An awareness of the whole as much as the parts. An awareness of the Quiet.

Of course, it's easy for me to describe it in these terms today. As a boy, I suppose all of the above was interesting but not earth-shattering. I remember making the connection between space and solitude, and observing the underlying quiet. I never forgot how some things are clear in the moment you observe them, but not when you look back and try to understand. But was that important? Was I the only one experiencing it? Was it like getting all excited about the vapor trail and not noticing the rocket? Sometimes I'd try to make sense of these things, but mostly I just went along with them. They were what they were. It wasn't until I went away to boarding school some years later that the significance emerged.

I'd moved from a world of quiet and isolation to one of rowdiness and (to my mind) overcrowding. From the calm to the chaotic; from natural space to mental space. But the remarkable thing was that, even in the midst of all this activity, I was only a few breaths away from the solitude and spaciousness I had enjoyed before. The difference was that now it wasn't nature producing it, but my own inner processes.

What a discovery. You could throw yourself into the vibrant, boisterous, competitive world of boarding school, then ease into the reassuring serenity of the Quiet when you needed to. They went hand in hand; one balanced the other. Excitement and calm. Achievement and peace of mind. Dynamism and the Quiet. I believed this was how life was meant to be. This was how it could be for everyone, wasn't it? I soon discovered that these were not the sort of observations my new friends and classmates cared about.

Perhaps the excitement would have waned had I not been introduced to a Thai monk at the end of one school term. He was teaching not far from my school. (I think he had visions of establishing a *sangha* in regional Queensland, but was hindered by lack of immigration status and local hostility to alien practices such as Buddhism.)

Thus began my introduction to formal meditation practice. It was not all that different from what I'd been doing all along. More important, I learned that what others got from it was the same sense of oneness and well-being that I had. I also learned that the moment-by-moment attentiveness I'd developed as a kind of entertainment was one of the ideals of Theravada practice. And, most surprising of all, nobody frowned when I tried to explain my observations of the underlying quiet.

The year or so that I attended his classes led to a lifetime of study of meditation and its possibilities—the different approaches to the practice, the common areas among them, and the different shades of consciousness they revealed.

## Just a breath away

Can you imagine a place so quiescent that the only sound you're aware of is that of your own breath?

When you hear it, your first instinct is to quieten your breathing. But you resist because there's an intriguing dimension to it. As you become more aware of the sound, you realize that it's not taking place in some remote part of your body, but is there inside your head. At your center. Now you understand why some teachers say the breath is the link between the physical body and the mind. More than any other aspect of your being, it's the ever-present link.

It's also the link between you and the Quiet.

Noises come and go. Ambient sounds fade in and out. But your breathing continues and the underlying quiet never wavers—for every moment of your life, these are the two constants.

# The instant replay posture

The following is about a simple posture that connects all the powerful feelings and emotions you create on your way through this book, so you can instantly play them back at any time in the future.

It's called **the Quiet reference point**, or **the instant replay posture**.

Before I explain how it works, spare a thought for Pavlov's dog. You know the story: each time Mr. Pavlov fed his dog, he sounded a bell; after a period of doing this, he could sound the bell and his dog would salivate in anticipation of being fed, whether or not the food was produced. In psychological terms, this is known as a *conditioned response*. It occurs when you subconsciously associate an object, touch, posture, place, or behavior with a specific feeling or impression. When you intentionally create a trigger that arouses this feeling, you have a *programmed* conditioned response.

It happens in two stages: first you make the association between the desired feeling and the trigger; then, when the association has become ingrained, you use the trigger to bring back the feeling.

We'll be creating several triggers throughout this book, but the handiest of them is this one. When you've perfected it, you'll have a quick and reliable way of changing the way you feel—from tense to calm, from steamed up to chilled, from overwhelmed to easygoing— without giving it a second thought. Then it becomes much more than a tool for your Quiet practices; it's something you can use in all parts of your life.

*The trigger we'll be using here is a posture. Lay the back of one hand in the palm of the other, and allow your thumb tips to touch lightly. If you're seated, rest your hands on your*

*lap in line with your lower abdomen. Now relax, and sense*
*the relaxed feeling easing through your body and coming to*
*rest in your hands.*

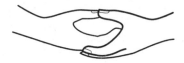

Perhaps you have seen this on Eastern sculptures and in paintings. It's one of the better-known *mudras* used in meditation. (*Mudra* is a Sanskrit word that means something like "gesture." There are hundreds of them, with purposes that range from improving health to channelling cosmic energy.) In Zen, this one is known as the cosmic *mudra*. Some traditions say that it encourages peace and introspection, while others claim it's a way of focusing your attention on the lower part of your abdomen so your oxygen flow is directed there.

The principle behind it is simple. When you are feeling deeply relaxed, you place your hands like this and, over time, you start to associate the two: a relaxed feeling with the posture. The more you do this, the more you build the association. Then, when it's firmly embedded in your subconscious, all you have to do is adopt the posture and you bring back the calm feeling.

Before you begin this, here's a way of making it even more powerful. It helps you change your mental state from intense and analytical into something that is soft and intuitive.

*Without looking down or moving your eyes, calmly direct*
*your attention toward your left hand as it rests in the*

*instant replay posture. Just relax and keep your attention focused there until all you're aware of is your left hand.*

*(Sometimes, especially if you're left-handed, you may find the reverse of this applies. Experiment with directing your attention to your right hand instead.)*

As each side of your brain is "wired" to the muscles on the opposite side of your body, you use your right hemisphere to focus on your left hand. The right brain is associated with imaginative, visual, emotive, and holistic processes, so you tend to feel more relaxed and easygoing when you use it. (There's actually a bit more to the story than this, but it works as I've explained.)

To keep the instant replay posture in mind, we'll use this symbol ⏝ as a visual reminder of the posture. This will prompt you to continue building the association with feeling calm and content. The more you practice it in peaceful moments, the stronger that association becomes. But they must be peaceful moments.

You can make it more powerful still. I once worked with a hypnotherapist who started all sessions by encouraging his patients to "wear the hint of a smile." It's obvious how this might work on a psychological level, but there's something more to it. It has exactly the same effect as relaxing your facial muscles. This leads to the whole body feeling more relaxed. When you soften the muscles in your cheeks and eyes, the edges of your mouth turn upward and your facial tension dissolves.

Just fold your hands as in the posture on the facing page, adopt the hint of a smile, and relax. To remind you of both of these, you'll see this symbol ——〜—— throughout the book.

## Building the association

Each time you're feeling peaceful, with everything in order, adopt the instant replay posture: wear the hint of a smile, fold your hands as shown, direct your attention to your left hand, and allow the association to build in its own unconscious way. Take your time. Do it often. Let it build.

You can do this anywhere. Sitting at your desk, in church, on the massage table, or on a park bench. For maximum effectiveness, choose places that are quiet and free from distraction. Then, when you're feeling restful and composed, adopt the posture. Pay particular attention to what it feels like. The more often you do it, the stronger the association will become.

## Applying the trigger

After you've built the association with the instant replay posture, you're ready to apply it.

Sometime in the future, *when you feel sure you've created the subconscious association between the posture and the feeling*, you can bring back that feeling just by adopting the posture. That's all. Leave the rest to your subconscious.

This is a powerful psychological technique that's also used in therapy, sports training, and personal development. By the end of this book you will be applying it to your meditation practice and other parts of your life as well.

# CLOSER TO THE QUIET

The fastest and most predictable way to access the Quiet is through meditation.

Raising this topic invariably invites debate. Is this style better than that style? Is this tradition better than that one? And so on. The Quiet practices sidestep these issues by taking a pragmatic, nonaligned approach. In other words, I've concentrated on what works best.

I've also drawn a clear line between the temporal side of meditation practice and the spiritual side. Book A is about the temporal side, Book B is about the spiritual. Both will dovetail with whatever style or spiritual direction you may already be following.

## Your intention

Generally speaking, the intent of meditation practice is to satisfy one or more of three quite different needs, all of which relate to the self: adaptation, exploration, and transcendence. Depending on your particular interest and stage of life, one will seem more important than the others.

## Self-adaptation

This is where you use the Quiet practices to help you cope with existing worldly situations. You might use them to address your stress or anxiety levels, to modify certain attitudes or behaviors, to manage pain, or to find some peace and quiet in a noisy, nonstop world. Many people have been drawn to meditation solely for reasons such as these.

## Self-exploration

This is where you use the Quiet practices for psychological purposes— to know yourself better, to understand the nature of your emotions and why you respond the way you do, and to explore deeper levels of consciousness. You might also use them as a vehicle for contemplations on fundamental questions about the nature or purpose of existence, or your relationship with the infinite (to use a general term).

## Self-transcendence

Depending on your point of view, this is either a step toward the ultimate goal, or the ultimate goal itself—enlightenment, divine illumination, liberation from the influences of the ego, self-realization, realization of the "not self," communion with God, becoming one with the cosmos, you name it. At its most basic human level, self-transcendence is when you stand back and become aware of the true nature of the self without the blinkers and distortions of ego. It's where you begin to see through the fog of everyday consciousness to reach higher realms of understanding. This is the spiritual dimension, where you discover those oft-spoken-about feelings of unity or sacredness.

No doubt one of these needs will seem more important to you right now. But don't become too attached to this, because your needs tend to change according to the stage of life you're at.

## The five worldly benefits

At the most basic level, the Quiet practices lead to improvements in your physical and emotional well-being.

Longer term, they always lead to some degree of personal transformation: at the deepest level, the person who sits down to meditate on day one will be different from the one who's sitting on day 300. And this seems to apply regardless of the needs that attracted you to meditation in the first place.

If you look at it from a worldly perspective, you find that the Quiet practices produce five benefits, to greater and lesser degrees. Some teachers may suggest others, but the benefits of meditation can usually be summarized within these five: peace, clarity, stability, lightness, and well-being.

**Peace** You were expecting this. After all, it's the most well-known benefit of all meditation practices. But this is not a state of rest we're talking about. It's a deeply satisfying state of mind, a state of *inner* peace. One that enables you to enjoy a sense of order and control while you participate fully in what life has to offer.

Contrary to what some claim, it isn't an immediate by-product of your daily meditation practice. It might flow from a reduction in your stress levels, I suppose, but it generally emerges as the result of two contrasting factors.

One is being able to stand aside. Regular Quiet practice allows you to spend time away from the "self" you present to the world and, perhaps, to yourself—so that your attachment to appearances, possessions, ego, desires, and so on eventually starts to fade. This not only releases you from a lot of pain, doubt, and emotional baggage, but finally allows you to feel at peace with who you really are.

The other factor is recognizing yourself as an integral part of the whole. One of the most common feelings to arise in meditation is frequently described as oneness: where you sense the interconnectedness of all things. Some describe this as a sense of oneness of body, mind, and spirit; or the feeling of being at one with all others; or the feeling of being at one with the universe; or the feeling of being at one with the supreme. However it is described, it's usually accompanied by a profound sense of inner peace and completeness.

When these two contrasting factors are realized—detachment and connectedness—a deep sense of inner peace becomes a fixture. You are at peace with yourself, the world around you, and whatever is happening. This is when the deepest spiritual experiences start to emerge.

**Clarity** The single greatest benefit you will derive from meditation is the ability to see what is.

Can you think of a time in your life when, just for a moment, the clouds parted, and everything became startlingly clear? This is very different from just having a bunch of answers. Suddenly all doubt vanishes. You have insight. You have depth of understanding. You have clarity.

Unfortunately, those illuminating instances are few and far between. While they sometimes come out of the blue, they're more common at turning points in life—such as when accident or serious illness strikes, or someone close to you dies, or you have a peak experience of some kind.

They also occur during the Quiet practices. Although rare, these moments of pure, uncluttered insight can be quite thrilling. Enough to shock you out of your reverie and make you start wondering, *How can I hang on to this?* But the instant you have this thought, you've altered your meditative state, and the insight goes. Of course, thrills are not what the Quiet practices are about. They're about cultivating the ability to see what is. Nothing more, nothing less. This can be a slow, incremental process. Or it can be sudden or serendipitous. But at the end of the day, all you get to see is what is already there. This can lead to a deepening understanding of reality and your relationship with it.

On the most basic level, clarity applies to your day-to-day view of life. This is a natural by-product of having an increased ability to focus or concentrate, and of having a calm, settled frame of mind. You know from experience that when you're stressed or under pressure, all you can see is the detail—the next hurdle, the problem before you, the thought that's most pressing now—and it's almost impossible to grasp the big picture. Conversely, when you're relaxed, with no deadlines or immediate pressures, it's much easier to form that overview. This is one of the reasons why people believe meditation helps you cultivate wisdom.

In the short term, this clarity is quite subtle—you'll have an increased ability to focus, you may be aware of sharper mental performance, and you may have the occasional meaningful insight. But after some time of regular practice, those moments become more frequent and predictable. This is not metaphysical; it's biological. It can now be shown that the practice of meditation permanently enhances the physical structure and performance of the brain, especially in terms of concentrative abilities, attention span, decision-making, and memory.

In time, instead of experiencing occasional flashes of insight, you find they stabilize and remain. They morph into a soft and diffuse awareness. Comfortable, like slipping into a warm bath. The change takes place so gradually that it may not be entirely noticeable to you. But, sooner or later, you become aware of it. And when you do, it's one of the most satisfying and unexpected aspects of long-term meditation.

Stability Another by-product of long-term practice is the way your overall mental state becomes more settled. This also happens gradually, though perhaps more noticeably than with the quality of clarity.

"Settled" can have a variety of interpretations. Some people describe it in emotional or subjective terms—as feeling more contented, more together or emotionally stable. Others liken it to becoming more resilient, more tolerant, and better able to cope with everyday problems. Some say that their thinking abilities grow smoother and more refined.

To some degree, this stability can be observed on a neurological level.

Whether this means a smoothing out of your brain-wave patterns, an ongoing increase or decrease in certain brain frequencies, or permanent change to the structure of the brain depends on the individual and the length of time you've been practicing. But measurable changes do occur, and they are often present after a relatively short period of using the Quiet practices.

**Lightness**  Call it lightness or spaciousness, this by-product of regular Quiet practice is something you might never have considered as a way of making life seem better. At its most fundamental level, it is experienced as a lightness of the soul or spirit. A sense of boundlessness and freedom. An ever-widening contrast between you and the weight of the world. Between you and suffering.

Even though that may sound kind of ethereal, lightness is also felt in unmistakably worldly ways. For example, some say that it relates to a range of physical improvements such as sounder sleep and more energy and alertness. Others describe it in emotional terms, such as an ongoing feeling of optimism or lightheartedness. I've heard it described as an awareness that there's room in your life for everything.

**Well-being**  There's no need to detail the many physical and mental benefits of regular practice—they've been covered in a hundred other books, including some of mine. We can summarize these benefits by taking a glance at the way your nervous system works. The autonomic system that governs your internal organs and involuntary actions comprises two linked systems: the sympathetic and the parasympathetic.

The **sympathetic nervous system** is designed to get you through difficult times by preparing your body for action. It speeds up your heart rate and blood flow, pumps "stress hormones" into your system, and arouses feelings of tension. The **parasympathetic nervous system** is designed to compensate for this. After the urgency has passed, it helps your body to return to normal. It calms, conserves energy, and helps your body to heal.

The Quiet practices replicate the actions of the latter. They help you to relax and unwind. They reverse many of the negative effects of stress, and they boost the efficiency of your immune system.

It's not hard to see how all of this might enhance your physical well-being.

Your emotional or psychological well-being is another matter. Generally, most of the psychological benefits flow from having a "settled" frame of mind. But how do these eventuate?

First, through **stillness**. In this day and age, almost everyone suffers from having too many things on their mind at any one time. The Quiet practices reverse this by narrowing your field of attention—either to one "object" or to a related group of them. This clears the mind of discursive thought, which leads to a powerful, restorative inner stillness. The immediate effect of this is relief from all worldly pressures and responsibilities, at least for the duration of your practice; in time, this spreads into the rest of your day.

Second, through **immediacy**. Another great emotional pressure of the current age relates to our obsession with time. Our concerns stretch over an impossibly broad field—from what happened way back when (manifested as regret, guilt, and overanalysis of past events) to what may happen in the future (manifested as fear, doubt, worry, and anxiety). This has the effect of limiting your ability to enjoy and appreciate exactly what is in front of you now. Today we focus more on "the completion of the job," "when I'm retired," "Why did I do that?" and "What will happen if . . .?" than we do on what's happening now.

The Quiet practices train your mind to be aware of the now.

Third, through **selflessness**. It would be fair to say that most emotional issues stem from our perception of ourselves. This happens in many ways, from the trivial ("Does my bum look big in this?") to life-defining ("I have an addictive personality"). But that's only the tip of the iceberg. No matter how honest we think we are with ourselves, we're acting out a story that we've created in our minds. Eventually this story becomes bigger than us, and we find we're trapped by the role of "Ashleigh X" or "Oliver Y," and there's no stepping back from it.

In time, the Quiet practices help you to see through the masks and pretenses of personality, to become more objective about your mental states, and to discover the real nature of the self. The essence of you.

## The three spiritual benefits

Every time meditation is discussed, there's the obligatory reference to its spiritual benefits. The assumption is that we all know exactly what those benefits are. But if you ask around you'll find that very few people outside of the mainstream religions can articulate any spiritual benefits at all—other than rote responses about happiness, inner peace, and enlightenment.

With so many different traditions and religions, involving hundreds of different types of meditation practice, you might expect to see a great diversity of opinion on the spiritual benefits. But when you narrow it down to the essentials, you are left with just three: meditation deepens your spiritual experience; it helps you to see through the myths and illusions; and it leads to transcendent apprehension of higher truth.

The Quiet practices deepen your spiritual experience by helping you to quiet the mind—so it's not so affected by the noise and distractions of everyday life. This brings a level of clarity that cannot be equaled by mental effort, rituals, fasting, or studying the scriptures.

Next, the Quiet practices help you to strip away the myths and illusions that you've been cultivating since childhood—so you develop an understanding of your true nature, and possibly the infinite. It does this by progressively helping you to appreciate that you are more than a body–mind, and are not just the activity of your thoughts.

Finally, each of the Quiet practices leads to a transcendent state of consciousness that reveals aspects of reality that you wouldn't normally be able to experience or comprehend.

Initially, these three benefits may not seem so important to you. However, if or when the time comes that they do, the steps you should take to achieve them are covered in Book B.

## The purpose

Now that you have an idea of their benefits, you may wonder whether the Quiet practices have some greater purpose.

It's curious how different schools and traditions follow ostensibly the same practice, yet vary so greatly when they explain its purpose.

When you are struggling to find a few moments' peace at the end of a working day, it might be hard to get excited about lofty purposes such as "experiencing pure consciousness" or "discovering the Ultimate Reality." You might be perfectly happy just to have a bit more peace and space in your life. Or to shed some stress and tension. You might be looking for meaning, or need a refuge from all the mayhem that's going on in the world. Maybe you're just curious.

If this is how you feel, then the purpose of meditation is just to be in meditation. You put aside the time, let go of the outside world, and be. No goals, no benchmarks, and no attempts to manage the event. Just be. Every day. Maybe twice a day. Sometimes with extraordinary depth, sometimes with lightness and pleasure, but with no other purpose than to be. Then everything else takes care of itself.

On the other hand, if you belong to a religion or have well-defined spiritual beliefs, you'll have a clear idea of what your purpose is.

Whether your intention is temporal or spiritual, you will eventually come to realize that it's not the meditation that has purpose, it's the practice of it. And in the longer term, you may well come to the conclusion that the purpose of this practice is *to train the mind so you have an ongoing relationship with the Quiet*. Regular practice gradually enables you to see through the myths and confusions of everyday life, and to experience and intuitively understand the spiritual nature of all existence. Your life will be different from that instant forward.

# The Quiet experience

If you're familiar with meditation methods, you'll have a fair idea of how the experience unfolds. But if you are new to meditation, the following question has probably been on your mind since the beginning of this book: "What exactly is meant to happen?"

The answer is . . . as little as possible. Some things do happen in the lead-up to the sitting, but nothing much is meant to happen during the sitting itself. The reason being that meditation is not an activity, it's a change in your state of consciousness. Just being, and observing, and going where it takes you.

Certainly, as a result of this, things will "happen." You'll feel more peaceful and contented. You'll see things more clearly. You'll feel more together. You may find your spiritual experience deepening, and start to shed some of the illusions you hold about yourself. And you may even have an experience of what some describe as higher truth, and what I've been referring to as the Quiet. All these are results of inner stillness or are experiences of awareness.

Even when you accept that nothing much actually happens during your Quiet practices, you'll still want to know what the experience is. If someone tells you it involves an altered state of consciousness, you'll naturally want to know what this feels like. The feeling is best left for other meditators to describe. Bearing in mind that no two people's experience is ever the same, here's a cross-section of their observations.

In the early days most people experience a comfortable, relaxed, maybe even serene state, interspersed by periods of restlessness. And the proportion of serenity to restlessness varies by the day and the individual.

After a few weeks or so, the experiences begin to vary.

Most people are aware of a feeling of security and contentedness. And, of course, peace. The intensity of these feelings varies from person to person—somewhere between profound and pleasant— but still interspersed by periods of restlessness. Some people say that this seems vaguely familiar, as if they've experienced it before.

After that, you get all sorts of interpretations of what is essentially the same experience.

I liked this description from a young student: "a simple feeling of innocence, how you'd imagine it would be like as an infant— loved, safe, no worries, happy, content." Some describe it in more passive terms: "empty, floating, detached." And sometimes you'll hear descriptions such as "radiant," "pure," "not aware that I'm meditating," "alive," "time stands still," and so on.

However, there's no such thing as an average experience. What you experience is what you experience. It will be different each time: you'll think it close to perfect sometimes, and frustrating at others. Considering that we're dealing with a subtle state outside the realms of everyday consciousness, this is understandable.

Besides, this vagueness will serve you well. Having any kind of expectation is an impediment to your enjoyment of it. The best results come when you forget what you've been led to believe about the experience, and just accept whatever arises.

The real power of the Quiet practices is not revealed until you stop trying to control your experience of them. Do your best to put your expectations aside, follow the steps ahead, and nature will take its own course. It does this elegantly and flawlessly—as long as you don't try to manage the event.

Deep meditative states, peace of mind, clarity, and stability will all occur. Changes will take place. But all in their own time. Everything is coming to light as it is supposed to. For your part, there is nothing you have to do except enjoy the steps ahead—for what they are, rather than for what they can do for you—and be open to what comes.

## A serene, altered state

Even though your experience of the Quiet practice is subtle and individual, the physiological state that accompanies it is more accessible.

It is possible to measure changes in brain activity, the variations in neurochemicals that affect mood and physiology, lactate levels, galvanic skin response, oxygen consumption, breathing rate, blood pressure, pulse rate, and so on caused by meditation.

Even the actual workings of your brain can be measured with medical technology such as magnetic resonance imaging (MRI) or, more commonly, with an electroencephalogram (EEG) (see www .evenmorequiet.com for more details). Both technologies clearly demonstrate what meditators set out to achieve:

- Decreased activity in the parts of the brain that relate to everyday activities such as work and thinking.
- Increased activity in the parts of the brain that relate to relaxation, holistic perspectives, insight, and self-awareness.

As the physiological state deepens, your brain's frequency patterns change even more, and the activity spreads between the left and right hemispheres. This is known as synchrony. In most of your daily life, activity happens on one side of the brain or the other. Usually the only times both hemispheres show a similar spread of activity is during meditation, perfect mind–body coordination, and those "aha!" moments of inspiration.

As you become more experienced you may begin to recognize the "feeling" of synchrony, and how it differs from other states. (Strictly speaking, it's not so much a feeling as an intuitive recognition of the state.) When this is really familiar to you, the mere recall of that "feeling" quickens the transition to the meditative state.

Yet as rare as it is, the meditative state that creates this synchrony is a perfectly natural human occurrence—more tranquil than the relaxed-but-wide-awake state you experience when you're lazing in front of the fireplace, but more aware than what you experience when you're in deep sleep. Your awareness is heightened; you're experiencing a sense of peace and personal integration, and in some cases you appreciate aspects of reality that are beyond the reach of everyday understanding.

More amazing still, you can produce that state right now by doing just one thing. *Stop thinking.*

The moment your mind comes to rest, your state of consciousness changes. You automatically start to ease into a deep, meditative state—one that's fundamentally identical to that produced by 30-year meditators.

But there's a hitch. Human beings can't consciously stop thinking. No amount of willpower or intellectual effort can directly stop a thought.

So you go about it in a roundabout fashion with processes such as the Quiet practices.

Instead of trying to stop thoughts, you fill your mind with something else. It might be one thing or a stream of things. A sound, an image, or everything that's happening to you at a particular moment. This prevents discursive thinking; and without the distraction of this mental activity, the mind comes to rest. Then you transcend your everyday state of consciousness.

## The art of letting go

Now we come to the first challenge in this book. While it's not a difficult one to grasp, it doesn't always come easily in our competitive, fast-moving world. The challenge is to let go of your need to manage what is ahead, and trust your own instincts to guide you to do whatever's necessary.

So for the next few pages, be prepared to allow things to happen at their own pace. Without applying effort. Without trying to analyze in any way. And without expecting any particular outcome.

If you're a manager or someone who's used to making your own way through life, it may not seem natural to participate wholeheartedly in something without applying effort, and without analysis or expectation. Yet that's exactly what I'm asking you to do.

**Without effort** seems an easy enough concept to come to grips with. We can all conceive of a pastime or activity where we do nothing, or almost nothing. Yet when it comes to mental activities such as the Quiet practices, we feel we should be *doing* something.

We're so used to directing and trying to manage what goes on in our lives that we've forgotten what it's like to just let things be.

Whenever you try to assert control over the natural ebb and flow of life, you end up either frustrated or disappointed—because it can't be controlled. Whenever you apply effort to trying to relax and slow down, you produce the opposite effect. Whenever you try to dictate the flow or the outcome of your Quiet practice, you negate its most wondrous benefit—the pleasure of simply being.

So get used to the idea of doing nothing, applying no effort, and just allowing things to happen and unfold in their own good time. However long it takes is exactly how long it's meant to take.

**Without analysis** also seems fairly easy to come to grips with. How many things do we do or participate in for the fun of it, without giving any thought to why we're doing them? Thousands of them. But when it comes to subtle matters of the mind or spirit, we can't seem to stop thinking about what's happening or, more pertinently, what's *not* happening.

The key to achieving the most from your mental states is to have a still mind. Being free from distracting thoughts. When you try to analyze the content of your experience while you're experiencing it, two things happen: your mind shifts into an intense, narrow, and detail-oriented mode; and your experience shifts out of the present and into the past. You cannot analyze anything while it is happening. Analysis is always retrospective—thinking about what has already passed.

The Quiet practices all take place in exactly the same moment. The one you're experiencing now.

There's another side to analysis that is equally important. As human beings we are desperate to rationalize and find the meaning in everything. *But there is no meaning to be found in the act of meditation*. Its purpose is just to still the mind so you can observe what is real. This will become clearer to you as you progress through the book.

**Without expectation** is possibly the most difficult discipline to apply. We expect a lot in life. We have been conditioned to expect it. We expect a lot of ourselves, others, the government, fellow drivers, public figures, priests, policemen, exotic dancers . . . When X happens, we expect Y to be the result. When we do good, we expect good in return. When we smile at a stranger, we expect them to smile back. For many of us, this expectation continues when we meditate. "If I meditate regularly, some sort of change should occur." "If I do it properly, shouldn't I be feeling different?"

Expectation only ever delivers a variation on what you expect— which blinds you to everything else that's going on. For example, if you walk down the street expecting to be accosted by beggars, in your awareness only one of two things will happen: you'll either be accosted by beggars or you won't. And your mind will be so full of beggars or no beggars that you'll be unaware of the warm sunshine and the fragrant blossoms on the trees.

Even more restricting, expectation means you have an emotional attachment to an outcome, which means you have a conscious or unconscious desire to exert control. It's not easy to relinquish control. Modern attitudes are geared toward immediate results, and big results. When our attention spans have been reduced to milliseconds, and the spectacular is more valued than the substantial, we eschew any course of action that has no obvious gratification or outcome.

The Quiet practices are at their most potent when you have no expectation, when you're open to everything, and when you maintain an attitude of naive fascination. Then you discover that not only is nothing expected of the experience but nothing is expected of you. There's no inherent responsibility. There's no right way or wrong way. You have the freedom to relax and enjoy what is happening *as it is happening*.

Then you realize that you are not using your practice to attain something, because the practice itself is the attainment. Impatience vanishes. You have all the time in the world.

**Without effort, without analysis, without expectation.** The three keys to making your practice a pure, life-enhancing experience.

*Turn your attention to this now. Just let go of everything momentarily. How does it feel to let go, and to allow things to happen at their own pace? Take comfort in the fact that there's no purpose in what you are doing other than to just be for a few moments.*

*How soothing does it feel when you discover there's nothing to think about? "Doing" is irrelevant. "Being" is everything. Being here. Being relaxed. Being present.*

*Maybe you've noticed how some changes are already taking place. Your vision is softer, your breathing is more relaxed, your awareness is becoming less cluttered, and your overall mental state is already more settled. And we haven't even started on the practice yet.*

*This is what happens when you pause ... without effort, without analysis, and without expectation.*

If you slip up for a moment and try to analyze this, you'll probably tell yourself it was just a psychological trick.

*But if you forget about analysis, and come back to the*
*present—just let go and experience whatever is happening—*
*you'll realize that much more is happening. You don't have*
*to do a single thing. And your state of consciousness is*
*changing of its own accord.*

# How the Quiet approach works

There are hundreds, perhaps thousands, of different meditation styles and approaches in use today, all urging you to head in slightly different directions. If you don't have the support of an individual teacher, how are you meant to know what's the right direction for you?

You'll be pleased to know it doesn't matter.

When you go to the core of all practices, the differences disappear. Strip away the rituals and historic artifacts, and they tend to follow the same pattern: the body influences the mind, the mind influences consciousness, and consciousness reveals spirit or the Quiet.

## body → mind → consciousness → the Quiet

You start with the body because it requires less effort to make a physical change than to change your state of mind. For example, most people can't switch from tense to relaxed through mental effort alone. But you can easily produce a more relaxed state of mind by making a physical change—such as modifying your style of breathing, or going for a walk, or just sitting there and have someone massage your shoulders. Where the body goes, the mind follows.

There's nothing new about this thinking. History's most influential shamans, salespeople, and hypnotists know that the fastest way to *positively* influence the mind is to start with the body. Many meditation teachers overlook this.

There are historic reasons for this. If you meditate in a dedicated environment like a monastery or ashram or retreat center, the peaceful surroundings will substitute for the body part of the sequence, and will have a direct influence on your state of mind. Similarly, if you're in a group meditation with a commentator pouring out a stream of peaceful, loving sentiments, the environment will do the trick. But if it's Monday morning in a noisy, buzzing city, you're going to need all the help you can get.

Because of this, all Quiet practices start at the beginning—using the body to influence the state of mind.

So if you can't rely on a monastic environment or a sweet-talking moderator to help you produce the desired state of consciousness or spiritual awareness, start with the body. If you want to streamline your practice to arrive at the desired state in the shortest possible time, start with the body. With the senses. With this moment.

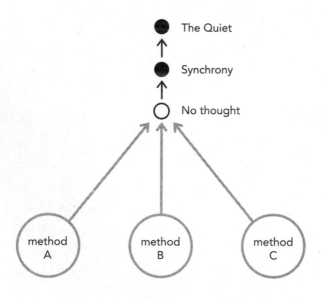

In a similar way, it takes much less effort to change your state of mind than to change your state of consciousness. There are many different meditation approaches that change your mental state, but ultimately they all lead to the same place of no thought. Or at least of no discursive thinking. When your mind comes to rest this way, you experience a synchrony of the right and left hemispheres of your brain, and the meditative state of consciousness. It is from here that you experience your relationship with the Quiet.

## The Quiet divide

Before we move on to the practices themselves, let's sort out an area of confusion that always arises in the study of meditation.

Regardless of the particular approach involved, there are two distinct components to the Quiet practice: one that relates to the physical world (A), and one that relates to the spiritual (B). These two components, or sides, are often lumped together into one subject for discussion or study. This produces many misunderstandings

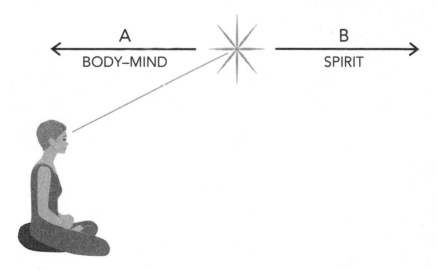

because, while one cannot exist without the other, the two have nothing in common.

This phenomenon is known as **the Quiet divide**.

In a typical meditation session, the A side is all about the physical and mental preparation and experience: the way you sit, the methods you employ, what you feel. All things being equal, this will lead you to the B side, the spiritual experience. At any given time you will be aware of A or you will be aware of B. At no time will you be aware of anything in between.

Most teaching, writing, and training focuses on the A side—the methods and disciplines of the practices involved. As this is the only side you have any direct influence over, you can understand why this would be so. But you might also see how this neglects the actual spiritual component of meditation practice.

Book A is about the A side of the Quiet divide—the worldly side—while Book B is about the B side, the spiritual side.

# THE QUIET PRACTICES

B ecause most meditation approaches share a similar core, I've been able to narrow the most important of them down to three. These are the Quiet practices of Deep, Directed, and Aware, renamed according to their core function, so there won't be any confusion or competition with the traditional methods.

In practice, the differences between these three approaches can be subtle. In intention, they can be worlds apart. Or at least this is so in the view of their advocates. In the end, though, each can achieve the same outcome. All take you to the same place.

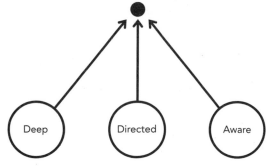

Individually or collectively, the Quiet practices train the mind so you can decide where to direct your attention. In your everyday state, you don't have much say in this: it's determined by what's going on around you. But with these practices you can tune out all the static and distractions, so your awareness is filled with what's happening in the present. This allows you to be in the very center of whatever you're experiencing.

Deep, Directed, and Aware do this in quite different ways. They're all about harnessing the attention, but they vary in how you do it. The best way to explain them is to use the analogy of a sky full of stars. **Deep** is when you fill your attention with just one star, and keep focusing on it until you are no longer conscious of any other. **Directed** is where you get assistance to focus on that one star. And **Aware** is when your attention is filled with all stars simultaneously.

# Deep

Deep narrows your attention. It is a concentrative or one-pointed style of meditation similar to that from the Yoga tradition, and is the oldest and most widespread practice of them all.

It focuses on a single object, action, feeling, word, phrase, or picture. This "object" can be meaningless, such as a candle flame, or meaningful (to the practitioner), such as a prayer or mantra. By focusing all of your attention on it, extraneous thought ceases and only awareness remains. Shielded from unwanted thought, worries and desires vanish, and you experience a beautiful, tranquil state.

Deep is the easiest practice to learn, requires the least effort, and is the one you will probably derive the most short-term satisfaction from. It's also the most direct route to the Quiet.

# Directed

Directed steers your attention along a specific path. Although similar to Deep, its main difference from the other Quiet practices is that it involves intentional thought. Where the others seek to reduce or eliminate thinking, Directed applies it in a structured way. This can either be self-directed—based on thoughts that you originate or entertain—or done with somebody else's explicit guidance.

Directed is similar to the contemplative practices in most spiritual traditions. The type of practices it can be compared with include spontaneous prayer, some aspects of Tantra, meditations on the names of the divine (various traditions), meditations on complex images such as a *mandala*, reflections on the scriptures, contemplations on historic events such as the Way of the Cross, Buddhism's Loving Kindness meditations, even the New Age guided fantasies that you thought you'd never have to experience again.

If you belong to a mainstream theistic religion or have a strong belief in a personal God, you'll find Directed is the most supportive. Many practice it religiously because it's recognized as one of the few ways to directly experience the divine.

# Aware

Aware broadens your attention. In some ways, this is the opposite of a one-pointed practice like Deep. Where Deep empties the mind, Aware fills it.

It's similar to the *vipassana* or insight meditation from Buddhism. With Aware, instead of focusing on one thing, you allow yourself to be aware of many, and so become fully conscious of every moment of life. In practice, you start by observing an aspect of your being—your breathing, bodily sensations, emotions, mental states, even your thoughts—but without judgment or analysis. This leads you to become aware of the true nature of such things as emotions, behaviors, and experiences, as they appear and fade from moment to moment.

Aware is a hyperaware state, not something dreamy or trancelike. So it leads quite naturally to extending your meditative practices into the wider world.

# All three in practice

It's best to experiment with each of these as you make your way through this book. After a while you'll recognize their individual appeal, and will see how different practices are appropriate at different times:

- **Deep** to condition the restless mind, and transcend everyday awareness, so that you encounter the perfect quiet of pure consciousness.
- **Directed** to deepen your spiritual practice and, for some people, to provide direct experience of the divine.
- **Aware** to train the awareness to be fully conscious of this moment. Learning to live in the present eventually leads to an intuitive understanding of the Quiet.

Some schools view these as alternatives. If you took that view, you'd settle on the one you feel most comfortable with. However, there's more to be gained if you use them in conjunction with one another—as a portfolio of Quiet practices. Later, you'll find out how.

| DEEP | DIRECTED | AWARE |
|---|---|---|
| inwardly directed | inwardly directed | outwardly directed |
| narrow | narrow | broad |
| you focus | you are focused | you witness |
| restricts attention to a single object | restricts attention to a stream of thoughts | attends to everything in a fresh, unconditioned way |
| empties the mind | fills the mind with one thing | allows the mind to embrace all |
| "merges" with the object of focus | communes with the object of focus | dispassionately witnesses all |
| object of focus fades | object of focus grows in dominance | everything is in constant transformation |
| overcomes thoughts and senses | overcomes extraneous thoughts and senses | aware of all sensory input, thoughts, and environment |
| tranquility | rapture | revealing |
| absorption | communion | hyperaware |

# Why they're called "practices"

There are individual meditation sessions (or sittings), and there is ongoing practice. While sittings can be pleasant and fulfilling, it is the ongoing practice that produces the benefits. Just like training for a sport or learning to play a musical instrument, the more you practice, the more intuitive your performance becomes.

The reasons for this are habit, kinesthetic memory, and change in brain structure. Habit you know. Kinesthetic memory is built by repeating a particular act or motion, until you move from "seeing-thinking-doing" to just "seeing-doing." But the last reason is the mind-boggling one.

MRI studies show that long-term practice of any discipline produces a change in the physical structure of the brain. The parts that relate to a specific action (such as the finger movements of a pianist or the swing of a golfer) literally increase in size.

Similar changes can be seen in the brains of long-term meditators, though here it is in the parts that relate to feelings of happiness and enthusiasm. Evidence of this physical change shows up in other areas as well.

It can now be shown that a person's brain-wave activity can be permanently enhanced through meditation practice—particularly in the way information from different parts of the brain combines to form a higher perspective or insight.

The most pronounced of these changes occurred in individuals who'd done 5,000 or more hours of practice. However, traits were evident after only a few months of meditation. Imagine there was a way you could accelerate this training period, and see those effects taking place much earlier.

The Quiet practices are designed to do just this.

Even though they speed up the process, and you start to enjoy the benefits from day one, the most profound results come when you accumulate practicing hours—time that you spend training the mind and the awareness. In some ways, this is like learning to fly or drive: you master the basic skills, then put in the hours to ensure they become ingrained. Once this happens, your actions become fluid, and intuition guides you more than intellect.

When you come to the Ongoing practices on page 155, you'll find there's a neat way of accumulating these practicing hours without having to sit around and meditate all day long.

Take care that this long-term goal doesn't become a distraction. The Quiet practices are not about outcomes, they're about participation.

## TURNING UP

A lot has been said and written about the way to get the most out of meditation. While all teachers have their own way of looking at this, there is one secret that tops them all.

It's turning up.

That's all. Just turn up, sit down, every day. Put aside the time—time you devote entirely to yourself—and don't give another thought to what's meant to happen. You'll have up days, down days, nothing-happens-at-all days. Sometimes more of one than another. But it's irrelevant. If you make a habit of just turning up, you accumulate sitting hours and sooner or later the change will have occurred. Then you'll wonder how it happened so quickly.

The fact that you are practicing is the goal, not what comes as a result of it.

In Zen they say that practice is enlightenment (as opposed to practice leads to enlightenment), and that the ongoing practice reveals nothing other than what is already there. It may take a while for you to fully grasp this insight, but turning up for practice each day is a great way to start.

There's no hurry. The leisurely pace of meditation is part of its charm, and the fact that it has no direct goals or outcomes removes the pressure.

## Linked by one breath

Soon you will discover that a subtle connection between all of the Quiet practices is the breath. While most meditation schools have at least one breath-focused method on their books, the connection goes much further than this.

The breath connects you to all living beings on the planet. It's the most obvious and intimate biological function in your life, one that you live with from the moment you're born till the moment you die. It influences your health, your emotional well-being, your physical and mental capacities, and even your spiritual development. Yet you seldom give it a second thought.

To ensure that you do give it a second thought, many spiritual, sporting, yoga, and martial-arts traditions emphasize breathing skills. Among the many reasons for this is the fact that moderating your breathing is one of the fastest ways of changing your mental state or the way you feel.

If you want to see this demonstrated, compare the behavior of a stressed person and a relaxed person. The stressed person breathes in short, shallow breaths; this limits the amount of oxygen for the bloodstream and the brain, which can lead to feelings of tension and nervousness. In contrast, the relaxed person breathes more slowly and deeply, which provides more oxygen for the bloodstream and the brain, and usually stimulates the production of relaxing neurochemicals such as endorphins. The conclusion: *you can change the way you feel and the way your brain works by moderating the way you breathe.*

To use the breath to produce a relaxed and positive frame of mind, all you have to do is take maximum oxygen into your lungs.

Try it now. Most people swell their chests and concentrate on the upper part of their bodies as they suck in the air. If you were doing this as you read, you would have felt your shoulders rise, your stomach suck in, and your chest balloon. That's okay, but it's a long way from optimum.

Try this alternative as a way of taking much more air into your lungs. Rather than lifting the shoulders or puffing out the upper chest, concentrate on sucking air into the *bottom* of your lungs, the diaphragm. If you place your hands on your lower abdomen, you'll feel your stomach rise as you breathe in.

This exercise seems easy to do when you're sitting here, concentrating. But how can you make it second nature?

One way is to practice the following while reclining.

Start by creating a rocking effect with your stomach muscles—stomach up as your chest falls, then chest up as your stomach falls. When you have a feel for this action, integrate it with your breathing. As you breathe in, note how your abdomen is rising. As you breathe

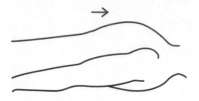 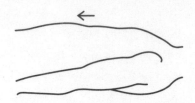

out, allow it to fall. Soon this rocking motion will be in sync with your breathing, and will feel relaxed and normal.

The next step is to regulate it. Breathe in for the count of three, breathe out for three. When you feel comfortable with this, increase the count to four. The object is to have inward and outward breaths of *approximately* the same length—so don't strain. Now you'll be taking maximum air into your lungs. Practice it for a minute or so when you wake in the morning.

*What does this have to do with the Quiet practices?* you may wonder.

For one thing, good breathing technique enhances your enjoyment of meditation. For simplicity and effectiveness, such methods have no equal—after all, you can't get more convenient than having the main tool of your practice with you every second of the day and night. And in most cases there's nothing in particular you have to do with it other than being aware that it's there. Wonderful!

Better still, once you begin to associate the breath with having a calm and clear mind, you can produce that state of mind by turning your attention to your breathing. Yes, you've created another Quiet reference point—an intuitive association between body and mind.

And you make it even stronger when you sit quietly and listen. The breathing sound appears to come not from outside, but from *inside* your head. Try it. Pause for a moment and try listening for yourself. There is no other physiological function that makes this body–mind connection so convincingly.

*Take a couple of moments to withdraw your attention from the outside world.*

*Without effort, without consciously changing timing or rhythm, and without any thought of doing it "properly," turn your attention to your breathing. Note how, just by paying attention to it, the air seems cleaner, cooler, and more refreshing. Note how each breath helps you to feel more peaceful and relaxed. Remember that feeling.*

# The principle of
# CenterWidenListen+Observe
changes your consciousness          what occupies your attention

Most meditation practices share a set of principles that have remained unchanged for centuries. **CenterWidenListen+Observe** is a summary of those principles. It produces the same results as traditional approaches, but in a more streamlined and contemporary way.

There are two components to it: one physical, one mental.

The **CenterWidenListen** part is about applying three physical steps to transform your state of consciousness—from the everyday into the meditative. The **Observe** component relates to what you fill your attention with once your mental state has been altered—this makes one practice different from another.

When you add the two components together you end up with a practice that's not much different from what comes from Yoga, Zen, Theravada Buddhism, Transcendental Meditation, Christianity, or Islam—except that CenterWidenListen+Observe is simpler.

The **Center, Widen,** and **Listen** steps are equally effective whether your intention is to meditate, to relax, to come up with a great idea, or just to escape from life's pressures now and again. They are so effective that some people ignore the Observe component altogether and use nothing but these three steps for their ongoing meditation practice.

## Center

The first step relates to centering your attention. It involves physical steps that help you withdraw your attention from the outside world and feel that you're in the center of whatever you are experiencing.

Most great performers intuitively seek to center themselves before a big event. You see actors and singers do this before they go onstage. Athletes, martial artists, soldiers, and surgeons do likewise—quietly trying to consolidate their emotions and energies before action.

There's something powerful and mystical about the center. It's the most stable part of a sphere. The center of gravity is the most stable position in any static object. The most potent force in nature (the strong nuclear force that holds the nucleus of an atom together) comes from the center. The most powerful positions in martial arts stem from the center. And it also plays a significant role in spiritual iconography.

So it should come as no surprise that the most serene and satisfying place to begin your Quiet practice is the center, or someplace you *feel* is the center.

Even if you did nothing else, this centering step would change your mental state. It's a gradual process, but it begins in less than a minute. There are three phases to it, which I'll describe separately. When you have perfected them individually, combine them into a single intuitive action.

The three phases are: breathe out, ground the body, then center the spine.

**Breathe out**  You've seen actors and athletes do this before they attempt any feat. Take a deep breath in; hold it a moment—as you tense your body—now breathe out forcefully! With that outflow of air, sense the pouring out of all your physical and emotional tension.

**Ground the body** Now turn your attention to where you're touching the ground or the floor. What follows varies according to whether you're using a chair or one of the traditional floor positions.

 *If you're using a chair*, stand for a moment and direct your attention to your feet, which should be shoulder-width apart. If you can feel them flat on the floor, focus your attention on three different points of pressure on your soles: the first on the flat part in line with your big toe, the second on the pad on the outer side of your foot, and the third in the center of your heel.

Sway a little to the left, then to the right—almost to the point of overbalancing—and you'll sense how these three points touch and seem to grip the floor. With this feeling firmly in your awareness, return to the seated position.

*If you're using a floor position*, don't bother about standing. Just sense where your buttocks and each knee touch the floor, so that these become the three grounding points. Sway a little to one side, then the other, until the triangular feeling is firmly in your awareness.

**Center the spine** The final centering step also has a direct influence on your state of mind. It's based on the understanding that you feel more relaxed and positive when your spine is straight, your shoulders are back, and your head is lifted.

You can use your imagination to make this physical action more relaxed and intuitive.

Imagine your spine is a string of beads, with one bead to each vertebra. Close your eyes and "feel" someone lifting that string, then gently swaying it from side to side. Move your body from side to side until you find the ideal resting place in the center. This is your center of balance.

Combine this with the grounded feeling we described above, and your body will feel centered, grounded, and stable—from the top of your head to the soles of your feet (or in your buttocks and knees if you're using a floor position).

## IN THE CENTER OF THE EXPERIENCE

When you use the above physical steps to create a centered feeling in your body and emotions, it's not such a great leap of imagination to move your attention to the very center of your meditation experience.

So whether you're focusing on your breathing, or on a tai chi movement, you can imagine being "in the center of the breathing" or imagine being "in the center of the tai chi movement."

This will become an important consideration in some of the Quiet practices ahead.

# Widen

The Widen part takes this one step further. When your body feels centered and you have a deep sense of being in the heart of things rather than on the periphery, your progress to the meditative state has begun. Now, let's continue the transition.

One of the discoveries I made in many years of neurofeedback experiments was how subtle physical changes—such as in posture or demeanor—can lead to big changes in mental state, particularly in inducing a meditative state of mind. Dozens of these were identified, the most intriguing of which involved using the eyes.

The most obvious is the simple act of lowering your eyelids. Or even partially lowering your lids. You already associate this with restful states.

However, the following method achieves the same result with two extra benefits: it produces a more inspired or creative state of mind, and it allows you to use it in public situations such as meetings or interviews. (You'll see the advantage in this when you come to the Ongoing Quiet practices on page 155.) Here's how it works . . .

Normally your vision *converges* at the point where your eyes focus. This is called foveal vision, and is what enables you to perceive depth and dimension. It is also a very narrow and detailed way of looking at the world. Most of your day is spent like this.

When your vision *deconverges*, your plane of focus remains the same but your view widens. Without moving your eyes, you take in more visual information around you. This is peripheral vision.

Not only do your foveal and peripheral visions present vastly different views of the world, they also produce vastly different types of understanding. One is narrow and detailed, the other is broad and holistic. Peripheral vision (and hearing) also is usually involved in creative insights and moments of inspiration.

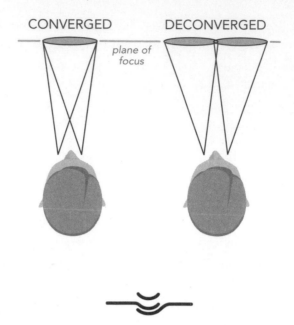

CONVERGED     DECONVERGED

plane of
focus

---

*Try it now. Fixing your gaze on something directly ahead of
you, without changing your focus in any way, allow your
peripheral vision to widen.*

*Without moving your eyes, gradually expand your
vision so you can take in more and more of the room
around you.*

*If it feels comfortable, you can take it further. Just relax
and allow your vision to widen ... until you can sense not
only the things beside you, but behind you as well. Now you
have a visual sense of being centered.*

When you allow your eyes to deconverge in this way, your brain-
wave patterns begin to change—from an everyday, detail-focused
state into something more relaxed and intuitive.

As you do this, you may begin to experience a number of subtle
physiological changes. The most obvious relates to your breathing—

did you notice how it starts to ease, maybe getting deeper and slower? And your facial muscles—did you notice how your jaw, cheeks, and forehead are feeling more relaxed?

You may be aware of psychological changes as well. Did you notice how you are suddenly aware of more going on around you? Did you notice how your internal chatter falls quiet?

**Deconvergence** is a powerful and versatile tool that can be used for more than the Quiet practices. For example, if you want to really hear what someone is saying, and extract more of the nuances from their words, instead of focusing intently on the speaker allow your eyes to deconverge. Now all your senses go to work. Or if you want to perfect an action that you've done many times before—a dance movement, say, or a golf swing—just let your eyes deconverge while your other senses play more of a role. Do the same if you want to find a more creative answer or solution.

The more you widen your vision, the more you involve your other senses, the more inclined you are to see the bigger picture, and the more restful your mental state.

## THE SOFT GAZE ALTERNATIVE

From time to time I meet people who struggle with the concept of deconvergence. If for some reason you don't find it as simple and intuitive as I do, try just *softening* your gaze. It has the same effect on your mental state.

Yes, it's slightly more visible to an onlooker (your eyes tend to have a glazed look), but you can learn to live with this. Just soften your gaze.

Now let's combine the two phases, Center and Widen, and see what it feels like.

*Breathe out forcefully, then allow your attention to drift inward, toward where you feel your center may be.*

*Sense the three anchor points where your body meets the floor. Note how these make the whole body feel grounded.*

*As you sit, imagine your backbone as a string of beads, seeking the most comfortable line to come to rest.*

*With the rest of your body now feeling centered and stable, allow your peripheral vision to widen. Don't try to force it or move your eyes, just allow it to widen so you take in more of what's around you.*

*Now relax and enjoy this centered feeling for a couple of minutes. Remember that feeling.*

Maybe you noticed what was happening there. The physical centering step helped to center the body. And the psychophysical widening one helped center the mind.

Now the last step—**Listen**—takes you the rest of the journey into a meditative state where body, mind, and spirit all are centered and as one.

## Listen

The way all of the Quiet practices work is by helping to settle the mind and develop an inner stillness, so you can become aware of the underlying quiet. If you don't have the skills to reveal this, it can be very elusive. You can't force yourself to notice it, because that would be counterproductive. The only way is to let go of your preconceptions and preoccupations, and just listen for it.

You can take this either literally or figuratively. To begin with, it's best to take it literally—to really listen with your ears, and consciously direct your hearing toward a sound. Later, if you wish, you can think of "listening" as being more of an attitude than a function. Then it becomes a state of not doing anything, but doing it with attentiveness. Listening to your true nature in a way that the normal hectic world does not allow.

In the Quiet practices, you'll discover there are two different ways you can listen—closely or widely.

**Listen closely** Most people assume that understanding is just a direct interpretation of the stimuli (such as light and sound waves) that your brain receives. It's more than this. Humans are dialogical beings—we use words and language to make sense of what's going on within and around us. Most of our thoughts, senses, feelings, and imagination are turned into words by a persistent little voice inside our head. This internal dialogue is continually labeling things, putting them into categories, and evaluating whether they are good, bad, or indifferent.

You think these words must be only in your imagination, right? Far from it. In the '60s, it was shown that a person's thoughts are accompanied by minute electrical signals in their vocal cords, and slight movements of the tongue. More recently, sophisticated recording equipment has revealed how these subvocalizations expressed in words—albeit in a mumbled fashion beneath the threshold of audibility—the very thoughts that a person later professed to be having.

You can see the downside to this. Words may be useful for sharing knowledge and impressions, but they are a major impediment to reaching the deeply relaxed states associated with the Quiet practices. Not only because of their persistent and intrusive nature, but also because of their volume: it's estimated that you often subvocalize between 200 and 500 words per minute, which is a lot of distraction.

Fortunately, there's also an upside.

Understanding the nature of subvocalization makes it easy for you to avoid it. We've already shown that if you could consciously stop the flow of your thoughts for a few minutes, you'd automatically drift into a relaxed, meditative state. But no one can do that. What you *can* do is consciously stop the flow of your internal dialogue, which has exactly the same effect.

To do this, just listen to the sound of your breath. Listen as you breathe in and out, but concentrate on the sound as you breathe out.

Why not concentrate on the sound of the inward breath, as some schools teach? You can do that if you wish, but it's nowhere near as effective in eliminating subvocalization. There's a simple, natural reason for this. In spoken conversation you deliver the words on the outflow of your breath: you pause as you breathe in, and you speak as you breathe out. To a significant degree, this also applies to your internal dialogue. Therefore, *by listening to the outflow*, you are focusing on the part of the breathing cycle where subvocalization would normally occur.

Try it for a few seconds now. See how quickly you start to feel more relaxed.

There's another reason why focusing on the outflow is more restful than focusing on the intake. Breathing in requires effort. A fair amount of energy and exertion is needed to extend your diaphragm, one of the body's largest muscles. However, it takes zero effort to breathe out. It's a simple act of letting go. Of release. It's the relaxing part of the breathing cycle.

Moreover, once you do let go in this way and your diaphragm muscles relax, the "relax" signals also affect the adjoining nerves, the brain cells associated with them, and so on. So it makes sense to focus your attention on the relaxing part of the experience rather than the energy-consuming one. Be aware of both the ebb and flow, but focus on the flow.

As your sitting progresses, your breathing will become light and gentle. Inaudible, almost. It will be flowing effortlessly, like a wafting breeze. Whether you can physically hear it or not is not important; all that's important is that you listen for it.

Try to imagine you are right in the center of your breathing, and just listen for it.

**Listen widely**  Sometimes listening closely to your breathing may be difficult—say, when you have a head cold. Here's an alternative approach that works just as well. It uses yet another peripheral sense, your peripheral hearing.

Are you surprised to read that you have peripheral hearing as well as vision? They work in a very similar way, and produce similar effects.

You can activate your peripheral hearing now. Instead of listening to what's going on close to you, listen for a sound that's way off in the distance. As far in the distance as you can hear. Take your time, don't force yourself to concentrate, and just listen for sounds farther and farther away.

Let your attention drift there now. Can you feel your state changing? Listening widely works almost as quickly as widening your peripheral vision.

## Three steps as one

CenterWidenListen is a proven way to speed up the early part of all meditation practices. While its primary role is as the preliminary stage of the formal Quiet practices, it can be an unobtrusive way of turning *all parts of your life* into a Quiet practice.

Later, you'll also be able to apply it to specific needs. Use it to steal a few moments of peace in a busy day. Or to gather your resources before you stand up before an audience. Or to clear your mind for an inspired thought when conventional methods fail.

CenterWidenListen is at its most powerful when you turn it into a habit.

Practice it in relaxed situations. Start for a minute or so at a time, then extend it when you find it convenient. Squeeze a few moments in wherever possible: in the office, on the train, waiting for the elevator. To make it even more ingrained, put aside a few minutes at the same time each day. Ideally, once after you rise, and, if you can manage, sometime before dinner.

When you can combine the individual steps into a simple, continuous action—where you cease to think about the parts, and are aware only of the whole—you'll be able to alter your mental state without closing your eyes, retreating to a quiet room, being seated, or using any out-of-the-norm techniques like visualization or mantra.

All you have to do is center your attention, widen your peripheral vision, and listen to the sound of your breath.

*Take a couple of moments to withdraw your attention from the outside world.*

*Recall how it felt earlier when your body felt grounded and centered. As you continue to relax, allow your peripheral vision to widen—so that you take in more of the room around you without moving your eyes.*

*Now, as you relax even more, turn your attention to the sound of your breathing. Listen as you breathe in and out, but pay particular attention to the sound of your breath as you breathe out.*

*Just listen to this for a minute or so, and note how calming that commonplace sound can be.*

## Observe

CenterWidenListen makes up the first phase of all Quiet practices—whether Deep, Directed, or Aware. The second phase relates to what you fill your attention with.

This is the **Observe** phase.

Conventionally, meditation urges you to "direct your attention," or "focus your awareness" on something in particular. This is meant to overcome the tendency to think.

Initially, most people struggle with these suggestions. Directing your attention or focusing your awareness are abstract activities that you never contemplate or undertake in your day-to-day life. You understand what they mean, sure, but they're not easily put into practice. They have another downside: they imply effort. They suggest that there is something you have to *do*. Even when you know this is not the intention, you have the subtle urge to act.

The Quiet practices get around these problems by substituting a step that is both meaningful and passive. So you can easily accomplish it, without feeling that you have to *do* something.

All you have to do is observe.

Each of the Quiet practices involves something different to observe. Observe without analysis and a remarkable thing happens: before you know it, your thoughts have come to rest, your attention is filled with the object of your attention, and you move even further into the meditative state.

**Attention or awareness** While we're on the topic of attention and awareness, it's worth noting the difference between them.

Attention is narrow. It involves a relationship between the observer and the observed—when you attend to one thing, you automatically exclude all others. Awareness is broad. In a worldly sense, it's the basic background knowledge that something exists or is happening—you have an awareness of something. In a spiritual or universal sense, awareness is closer in meaning to consciousness.

**Deep** *narrows* your attention so as to quieten the discursive, rational mind. To do this, it fills your attention with just one thing. If that one thing were the breath, the Deep formula could be summarized as "CenterWidenListen, then Observe the breath."

**Directed** also narrows your attention. But instead of focusing on only one thing, you focus on a stream of words or thoughts that leads you to the object of your meditation—God, universal consciousness, loving awareness, or whatever you choose it to be. So the formula for the Directed practices might be "CenterWidenListen, then Observe this stream of thoughts."

**Aware** *broadens* your attention so you're acutely aware of all that's happening as it happens. This helps you to experience every aspect of life with freshness and innocence. So, broadly speaking, the formula for the Aware practices might be "CenterWidenListen, then Observe what's happening in this moment."

# The most profound moment ever

I know you're going to let it slip if I don't draw special attention to this piece of essential knowledge: *the most critical aspect of the Quiet practices relates to the duration of your effort.*

It has no duration.

The one thing the entire universe experiences simultaneously and identically is this moment. Think about it. It's pure awareness. It's only when we pause and reflect (that is, after the event) that the differences emerge.

In the martial arts, you're told that strength and dexterity come from being present—not thinking about what your opponent has done or may be about to do, but remaining focused on now.

When you are completely focused on this moment, there is no movement of thought. There is no opportunity to think of the past or future. Hence, they do not exist. So simply being present equals no thought.

When you are focused on this moment, you become wholly aware of, and open to, what you are experiencing. It can't be compared with anything you've experienced before (reflection), or evaluated according to what you might experience in the future (projection), or analyzed according to whether this is the correct way for it to be unfolding. Therefore, pleasurable emotions like love and happiness can only be experienced now.

When you focus on the present, you eliminate anxiety, fears, doubts, and worries (future), all time pressures (future), and all guilt and regret (past). When you are focused on this moment, everything happens from an innocent, unconditioned, unmediated viewpoint. The notion of "from this moment on . . ." is inconceivable. The belief that "something needs to happen before [I will be happy, content, satisfied, enlightened, or whatever]" no longer holds water. This moment is all there is. It would be a pity if you overlooked it because you were thinking about something else.

Sometimes it helps to put it into words that "this is the most important moment in my life." Try saying it to yourself now. Then experiment with the following.

*Pause for one moment. Withdraw your attention from the outside world and allow it to be totally focused on this page. Only the words you are reading. Ignore everything that is happening around you other than the transmission of meaning from this page to you.*

*As you do this, you find the external world begins to recede. You find time is ceasing to have the meaning it used to. Some people think the present is where past and future intersect, but you are now discovering the opposite—that the past exists in this present moment, the moment you are thinking about it. The same with the future. Imagine how liberating it is when you come to realize, and accept without analysis, that both past and future are activities of the present.*

*The present is all that exists. It is all that will ever exist. When you are in the center of an experience in this present moment—as you are as you read these words—time doesn't exist in the conventional sense. This moment is without dimension or duration. With no beginning and no end. It's the one instant in life when past and future are beyond care or awareness.*

*This is the one moment when you can enjoy peace of mind and contentment. When you can enjoy an intuitive understanding of the Quiet. When you can feel happy and fulfilled.*

*And—did you notice?—you are enjoying these feelings right now.*

Each of the Quiet practices is designed to take place in one moment only. Just one moment. Then you become wholly engrossed in a "now" experience, one of novelty and nonappraisal. Now every meditation experience is unique, and incapable of disappointing because it cannot be compared with another.

As a moment-by-moment event, rather than a this-leads-to-that type of experience, whatever is taking place must be perfect in its own right. Because that's the way it is. It cannot be changed. There is no other way it can be.

Now you experience every moment, every breath, as if for the very first time. An endless succession of very first times, every moment like waking for the first time. Like arriving at a wonderful new destination for the first time. You experience it as something you have never experienced before, and will never experience again. You enjoy it for what it is—not for what it means. When the true realization of this occurs, you are making life's most illuminating discovery.

And, yes, it's happening right now. In this very moment.

# The physicals

Before moving on to the nuts and bolts of the Quiet practices, the final housekeeping matters relate to the physical specifics of place, posture, and period.

# Place

Have you ever noticed how you associate certain places with certain feelings? When you walk into a dentist's office, your nerves are on edge. When you walk into an ancient temple, you feel calm and relaxed. This is known as a conditioned response, similar to what we covered on page 26.

Most meditators have their own special place to which they retreat for practice. This could be a favorite chair, a favorite corner, or a favorite room. Sometimes they add pictures, candles, incense, soft lights, etc. Some allow for music. Others include sacred objects or religious pictures. Some even have specially constructed altars. Over time, the meditator builds such a powerful psychological association with this place that they start easing into a meditative state just by moving there.

My meditation place is dominated by practical items like soft lighting, carpet, a chair, cushions, a blanket, and a range of meditation shawls that have been given to me over the years. (Your body temperature drops while you're meditating, so it's a good idea to have a shawl or wrap.)

For visitors and students I have a collection of *zafu* (seating cushions), *zabuton* (padded mats), and *seiza* benches (small wooden meditation benches used in Zen practice)—these are relatively common items from yoga shops, and are useful if you use any of the floor positions.

# Posture

The key postural element for seated meditation is stability. Straight back and good airflow come next. Comfort comes last.

Stability arises from the three anchor points that we covered in

"Center" on page 65, and from having a straight back. But straight doesn't mean rigid. The object is to facilitate an easy flow of breath by opening up the chest cavity, which can only be achieved with a straight back. This also keeps you alert, and is a good way to prevent dozing.

As long as your body is relaxed and your back straight, whatever seating position you feel comfortable with is fine.

The classic meditation postures are the cross-legged floor positions associated with the Yoga tradition. If your flexibility is up to it, they have a lot to offer. The **Lotus** is the benchmark, considered to be the perfect meditation posture. Seated on a cushion with your two knees touching the floor, your head and neck will be in line with your spine, and you will find it easy to remain stable and alert. But it does take practice, and it's not for everyone.

A more comfortable alternative is the **seiza** posture, the kneeling position used in the Japanese martial arts and Zen meditation. It's the one you see in tea ceremonies, samurai movies, *shakuhachi* (flute) performances, and so on. It's designed to naturally align your body and spine, and to maintain a restful state of alertness. It's easier to

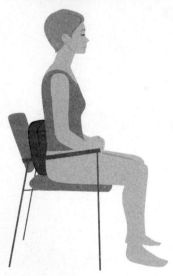

master than the Lotus postures, easier on the joints, and more energetic in nature. (Lotus postures are sometimes known as "stillness within stillness," and seiza is something like "potential for action within stillness"—as you'd expect from a posture related to the martial arts.) This posture may be more comfortable if you use a wooden bench or sit on a cushion between your legs.

If you prefer a chair, try to sit forward so your spine remains straight without a backrest. A low cushion between you and the chair back may help. Ensure your feet are flat on the floor, and your thighs parallel to it. If the chair height doesn't allow for this, rest your feet on a cushion or get a smaller chair.

If you are bedridden, it is okay to meditate while reclining—although it's best to avoid this at other times, as there is a tendency to associate it with sleep.

Once your posture is sorted out, you might start to wonder what to do with your hands. The basic hand-smile posture covered on page 28 is as far as you need to go. There are many others, but their subtlety eludes me and I've yet to meet anyone who will attest to their usefulness.

Finally, we come to the eyes. Most meditation takes place with the eyes closed. Because you associate this with rest, and it cancels out your most dominant sense, closed eyes automatically lead toward a meditative state.

Some schools encourage you to practice with your eyes open, or slightly open. To begin with, it feels a bit awkward to meditate this way, but it does have its advantages. Not only does it keep you awake, it stops the mind from wandering so much—a good thing to know for those times when your mind refuses to slow down. If you meditate this way, make sure you continue to blink as usual.

## Period

Now we come to meditation's biggest hurdle, but the most easily overcome—the amount of time you devote to it. Have you ever said, "I'd love to meditate, but I don't have the time"? Or "I used to meditate, but couldn't find the time to continue"?

One of the major advantages of the Quiet practices is how easy it is to find the time for them.

Initially, all you need to find is 13 minutes. In time, you'll think of ways to squeeze further moments out of your day, without sacrificing any of the things you love to do.

Also, the question of "How do I know when the time's up?" usually arises. It's easy to keep a clock or watch nearby (not on your wrist), but even easier to put your faith in your instincts. If you are convinced of your own innate timing abilities—and it's all a matter of trust—you'll open your eyes on the dot of 13 minutes, every time.

# The flow of a Quiet sitting

Now that you know the principles involved in the Quiet practices, let's see how they apply to a sitting.

In an ideal world, this would be something to discover from your own experience, just taking things as they come, without effort, analysis, or expectation. But in today's world, we've been detuned to subtleties like meditation, so sometimes a bit more preparation is required. So, in the broadest possible sense, this is how the Quiet practices flow.

In the early days of your practice the pattern is fairly consistent, regardless of whether you are sitting for 10 minutes or 60 minutes. It incorporates four distinct phases, each of which is characterized by a specific pattern of brain-wave activity.

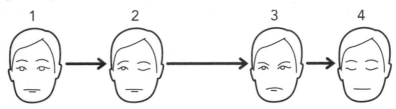

The initial stage (1) is where you are relaxed and getting ready. Stage 2 is the settling-in, or moving into the meditative state. Some people think of it as the distraction part: you've followed the steps to the letter, you've been sitting in your quiet place for some time, and the only thing you are aware of is the number of thoughts you've been having. "Am I doing it right?" "Nothing's happening." "How long has it been?" "When I finish, I must go to the supermarket . . ." Even the most experienced meditator experiences this. The difference is the duration, which varies according to circumstances and the attitude of the meditator.

Whatever is going through your mind at this point, more-influential things are happening to the rest of you. You'll be exhibiting visible signs that you are becoming physically relaxed. As long as you do nothing to inhibit it, this process will continue of its own accord. You probably won't even notice the subtle physical changes taking place—your pulse rate slowing, your breathing becoming slower and more relaxed, and any thoughts becoming further and further apart. Even if you think there's a lot going on in your mind, you are moving slowly and predictably toward the meditative state (Stage 4).

But something happens. The instant you become aware of the fact that something is changing, you start to analyze. In a flash, your everyday conscious mind reasserts itself (Stage 3) and, instead of moving deeper into your meditation, you are trying to make sense of what was taking place.

I remember this phase well from meditation in my mid-twenties. It hardly existed in my childhood—in the quiet of the outback I was happy to move from one stage to another without needing to know what was happening. But as I matured I grew more analytical and demanded answers. For a while, this became a barrier to my moving into the deeper stages of meditation. Fortunately, once you let go of the need to analyze, the journey automatically continues.

However, it's not always mental activity that defines this point. It may be a burst of restlessness: an itch, the urge to cough, feet that need shuffling, growing impatience, or a glance at the clock. Other times it may be a jerk or spasm. On rare occasions, it could be an issue from your past, such as unresolved grief or something to do with a relationship.

All meditators experience this restlessness. The difference is how they respond to it. Beginners give in to the distraction, then find themselves back at the settling-in stage. Experienced meditators

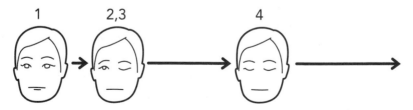

recognize it as the transition to deeper states. There is always a choice: give in to the restlessness, or continue the journey.

As you grow more experienced, you'll hardly notice the early stages, and most of the time you'll move fairly directly into the meditative state. The Quiet practices are designed to accelerate this, and make it as smooth and as effortless as possible.

Whether it takes 30 seconds or 10 minutes to get there is irrelevant. If you are taking it moment by moment, you'll find satisfaction in whatever happens.

## A NOTE OF CAUTION

With any form of meditation, you're dealing with the most subtle aspects of your mind. You also induce a range of physiological changes. Although rare, it's possible for some people to have adverse reactions to these.

If at any time you feel uncomfortable with what is happening, or feel something isn't right, just stop. Either put it off until another day, or consult a qualified teacher.

If you are currently receiving psychological treatment, or are on medication of some sort, see your therapist.

If you feel that anything might be detrimental to your physical or mental health, just stop. Talk it through with a health professional.

And if you'd like to meditate and, for one of the above reasons, you cannot, just use the Ongoing practices beginning on page 155.

# QUIET PRACTICE 1:
# ⊕ DEEP

D eep is a concentrative or "one-pointed" style of meditation. The principle behind it is that by focusing your attention on only one thing, you gradually exclude all other stimuli from your consciousness.

When this one-pointedness occurs—that is, your mind is occupied by only one thing—you will be in a state of full awareness, yet free of all discursive thinking. This produces a unique state of consciousness that is the exclusive domain of meditators. In addition, this brings a raft of psychological benefits, not the least of which is a settled, orderly frame of mind.

We're going to explore the Deep practices in a number of different ways. The first is fairly elementary, but it's essential to the cultivation of a sound, lifelong practice.

# NOT ENOUGH TIME?
## TRY 13 MINUTES . . .

Most long-term meditators spend an hour or so each day in the practice. Often much more. You might view that as an impossible commitment. If you're already burdened by how few hours you seem to have in the day, taking some of this for meditation might seem like a fantasy.

With this in mind, I set out to find the briefest possible way to enjoy the benefits of meditation.

Traditional approaches are pretty inflexible. They are based on the assumption that you have plenty of time at your disposal or will find whatever is necessary.

Once you commit to that, the belief is that the results will come when they come.

Conventionally, you start by sitting for half an hour, twice a day, and gradually extend this to an hour or longer. Sounds daunting, doesn't it?

The Quiet practices are designed to take up less of your time—until you decide you would like to extend them. You continue with these short sittings until you feel the benefits cutting in. Then you use *these benefits* as the motivation for extending your practice when you're ready.

The starting point is to ensure you're feeling the benefits relatively quickly.

Although short-term results are not what the Quiet practices are about, they will help you realize the bigger goal of creating an inspiring lifetime habit.

# 2+10+1

A 13-minute Quiet practice is all you need to start with:

- 2 minutes for letting go of the outside world, then the CenterWidenListen steps.
- 10 minutes for the Observe step, the practice itself.
- 1 minute at the end, to do nothing but luxuriate in the relaxed state you've created.

The advantage of 13 minutes is that it's easy to find. To put it into context, that's how long it takes you to make a relaxed cup of tea and drink it. And what makes it even easier is that this is not 13 minutes of effort or duty, it's 13 minutes of indulgence. Of peace. And quiet. And space.

Thirteen quiet minutes. Where you won't be disturbed. Where the phone is off the hook. Where all you have to do is sit back and focus on your own peace of mind.

EVEN MORE PLEASURE

How about finding two 13-minute packages in your day? One after you rise (get up 13 minutes earlier, if you feel it won't fit into your schedule), and one later in the day.

Thirteen peaceful minutes, twice a day. Just like having two cups of tea. If you can find more 13-minute breaks, even better. Take as many as you can find. We're trying to create a habit here, and the benefits of all these small breaks is cumulative. If you can manage this every day, great. If not, do the best you can.

# A deceptively simple process

Now that you have an idea of how a Quiet sitting flows, you may want to explore the process that enables it.

When you set out, your mind is full of thoughts. These are restless by nature, moving from one topic to another in a dynamic and largely unpredictable pattern. So while you might start out thinking of breakfast foods, you could soon be thinking of waistlines or dentists or train schedules. You can't overcome this restlessness through mental effort. But you can sidestep it by focusing your attention on an "object," such as the sound of your breathing.

Initially this works, and you have only breathing on your mind. But after a while more thoughts arise and, before you know it, you're thinking of train schedules and breakfast foods.

When you become aware of this, you calmly redirect your attention back to the sound of your breathing. Sooner or later, all extraneous thoughts will cease, and there'll be nothing on your mind other than the object. Your attention will have "merged" with your breathing. As basic as it sounds, this can be a blissful and revealing experience.

Is this a sustainable feature of your meditation? Not for some time yet. How long does it last? Who knows? And because it's all happening on a moment-to-moment basis, you'll have no idea either. It's only when your state of consciousness returns to the everyday—such as when you start thinking and analyzing again—that you become aware of the passage of time. The beauty of the Deep practices is the way they make time stand still.

As the name implies, Deep~By Numbers is an introductory level. If you're new to meditation, or are reading this for a more balanced view of the topic, there'll be an obvious appeal in this. However, if you're an old hand at this—say, you're a lapsed meditator or have had long experience in one tradition and are curious about others, or are not getting much satisfaction from your present practice—you may think you're going over old territory. That may be. But it will be enjoyable territory, and it's a good way to shore up the foundations of your practice.

# Deep~By Numbers

Even though I've described this as an introductory-level practice, that is not a reflection on its depth or potential. It's very powerful, and very efficient. There's no reason you couldn't use it for the rest of your life, and derive all of the benefits that I've promised.

If you've established a quiet place for yourself, now is the time to put it to use. Take the phone off the hook, kick off your shoes, and make yourself comfortable.

First we're going to follow the three CenterWidenListen steps described on pages 64–75. This starts to change your state of consciousness from the everyday into the meditative. Following that comes the Observe stage, where you make the act of listening to your breath even more mesmerizing.

CenterWidenListen *Take a couple of minutes to let go of the outside world, to Center yourself, and to allow your peripheral vision to Widen. Then, when you're settled and your body is relaxed, Listen for the sound of your breathing.*

Observe *Observe the sound of the breath as you breathe in and out, then count the outflow of each breath as follows.*

*Breathe in. As you breathe out, hear "one" spoken softly in your imagination. Breathe in, then hear "two" on the out breath. Continue for 10 breaths, then start again.*

*Keep this going for 10 minutes.*

*Really observe that breath, and count "one," in the moment it occurs. Observe the next breath, and count "two," in the moment it occurs. Don't evaluate or analyze or think ahead, just observe the breath in the moment it occurs.*

*There's no need to emphasize your breathing in any way. It's not important that you actually hear it. Just listen for it, and count.*

*If random thoughts arise—which they will—calmly redirect your attention to your counting. Soon you'll have increasing periods of no thoughts, where your awareness is filled with the sound of your breathing. Remember, this is a moment-to-moment exercise. There's nothing to analyze or think about: no other moment to compare it with, and no other moment to look forward to. There is only this one. For better or worse, just accept and enjoy it for what it is.*

*When it's all over, sit there idling for a minute or so, and stay with that relaxed feeling. That's all there is to Deep~By Numbers.*

## Deep tomorrow morning

Now it's time to start putting Deep~By Numbers into practice. Practice means doing it regularly. Ideally, that means every morning from tomorrow on. And at least one other time during the day—such as the evening, or whatever other time is convenient. Practice means creating a habit. If you can, squeeze in several sittings—even if they are shorter than the 13 minutes we mentioned. It's all habit-building.

For most people the morning sitting is the most important. It starts your day in the best way possible: in a calm, positive, orderly frame of mind. After you get used to this, you'd never think of starting your day in any other way. It's like combing your hair or brushing your teeth.

"But you don't know what it's like," you may say. "I have a wall-to-wall schedule as it is. How can I fit anything else in?"

Millions manage it every day. But if you can only manage a few times a week, that's fine to start with. Once you begin, finding time becomes much easier than it seems right now. My personal practice varies between one and two hours a day, even during the busiest periods—writing books, conducting research programs, running businesses, raising a family. It's easy to find the time for the things you love.

If you believe your schedule is overloaded, a subtle shift of view-point is usually all it takes to change. For a start, 13 minutes is a make-yourself-a-cup-of-tea-and-drink-it interval; you can easily find that. If not, rise 13 minutes earlier. After the second day you won't even know it's missing.

"But I'm not a morning person . . ."

I wasn't either. You don't have to change the way you are. All you have to do is find a few minutes in the morning to listen to your breathing. If that means rising 13 minutes earlier, you'll get used to it. If you think of this Deep practice as a way of catching a few quiet minutes to yourself each day, with the possibility that the benefits will come when they come, you'll always feel rewarded. Put the benefits out of your mind, and focus on building the habit.

So tomorrow morning is it!

If you haven't already begun, this is the beginning of an adventure. A lifelong practice.

The first steps will be subtle. You won't notice much of a change for the first few weeks or months. But in six months' time you'll look back and see a succession of improvements. You'll look at a cloud in the sky and think to yourself, *I've never noticed how beautiful clouds are.* You'll find yourself talking to someone you'd never normally notice, and realizing what an extraordinary being you're relating to. You'll find yourself breezing through ultra-busy days without feeling stressed and pressured. You'll experience all the usual ups and downs without taking it so personally.

And if you look back in five years, you'll still be the same person—same strengths, same weaknesses—but on the inside you'll have changed. Forever.

I've tried to be modest about the claims up to this point, but what you are already involved in is the single most important venture you will ever undertake. Neither birth, death, nor any event in between is as important. By the end of this book you'll understand why. This has nothing to do with the minor benefits we've spoken of—alleviating stress, helping you to sleep better, improving your immune system, etc. This is about the big things. Why am I here? How should I live? How can I have ongoing happiness?

Tomorrow morning, you take another bold step toward having answers to these questions. Toward finding real peace of mind and contentment. Start again tomorrow.


## The natural hindrances

All Quiet practices have their ups and downs. Sometimes you can be thrown off track by the downs. The following are the most common distractions to successful meditation. They relate not only to the Deep practices but to the Quiet practices in general. *Before you go through them, reread the Note of Caution on page 86.*

**Expectation**  Sometimes it's hard to come to grips with just how uncomplicated this Deep practice is. It's also hard to avoid trying to find the meaning in it. From time to time you'll find that it doesn't meet your expectations—"There must be more to it," "I might be doing something wrong." This is why it's important to bypass your expectations and just focus on enjoying the few minutes of peace and quiet you've allocated yourself.

**Impatience**  An uneventful activity like Deep is a natural target for impatience, especially if you're feeling under pressure. Unless you learn to really let go of the outside world for the duration of your sitting, you'll find impatience grows in line with the amount of pressure you feel under. There's a certain irony here, because meditation is so often used as an antidote to stress.

The early-morning and end-of-day routine is one way to avoid impatience, but the best way is to allow yourself plenty of room in your schedule. If you squeeze 2+10+1 minutes into a day of chaos, impatience may get the better of you. Better to play around with the formula a little—add more "getting-in-the-mood" time prior to your practice. Experiment with 3+10+1, or even 4+10+1, until you find a timing that suits.

**Thoughts**  No matter how experienced or disciplined you are, thoughts will arise in your Quiet practices. This is not a failing. They are part of meditation. In fact, they're an essential part of your practice.

Because *it is the moment that you recognize you're thinking, then go back to listening to your breath, that you strengthen your practice.* Just like an athlete training with weights—it is the resistance of the weights that builds his strength, not the lifting of them. In meditation it is the recognition of intrusive thoughts, not the avoidance of them, that makes the difference.

From another viewpoint, some believe thoughts are the body–mind's way of shedding stress, and that their presence is an indication this is happening.

In a general sense, the best way to deal with uninvited thoughts is to treat them with indifference: *Yes, it's a thought. Now, back to listening to the breath*. Your task is just to observe the sound of your breath, not to eliminate thoughts. The fact that they may be stilled as a result is incidental.

Thoughts come, thoughts go, and it will always be this way. If you treat them with indifference, they'll pass without involving you in any significant way. Because it is not the presence of thoughts that impedes your meditation, it's your *engagement* with them. If you hang on to one, or entertain it, or let it take you to another topic, you're involved in thinking, not meditating. But if they arise in your awareness and you pay them no particular attention, you continue to meditate. It's like observing a flow of people past your window— they come, they go. It's only when you call out to one, or dash out into the street to see what they're wearing or where they're headed, that you bring them firmly into your consciousness.

Trying to force thoughts out of your consciousness is pointless; it has the opposite effect. When they arise, allow them to be. As if they were somebody else's, and you were an uninvolved bystander. When you become aware of them, gently shift your attention back to your breathing.

Another common side effect of meditation is how you find yourself beset by inspiring insights—creative ideas always come from relaxed minds. While it's tempting to get involved with these, the ideal is to let them go like any other thought.

But what if a real gem comes along? Or something really important? Just opening your eyes for a moment is usually enough to embed it in memory so it can easily be retrieved at the end of the sitting. (Yes, it is considered poor form by the meditation establishment. But the traditional schools weren't designed for busy modern lives. It's hardly worth losing sleep over an occasional interruption.)

**Tiredness**  Physical tiredness is possibly the major impediment to your Quiet practices. When you're tired, it's difficult to focus, your awareness is dulled, and you may find yourself moving toward and away from sleep.

Meditation is not a sleeplike state, nor is it characterized by numbness, drowsiness, or sleepiness. On the contrary, during it your awareness is at its most refined. So you enjoy it more when you are well rested.

Go to bed an hour earlier if you need to, and practice at times of day when you're feeling most awake. Also, avoid using too comfy a chair.

**Breath-related issues**  One of the reasons I recommend focusing on the outflow of the breath rather than the inflow is that it removes the tendency to moderate the way you breathe. Nevertheless, it's possible that someone might become agitated or restless as a result of concentrating on their breath.

Should you ever feel this way, simply forget about the breath altogether, and use the visual approach on pages 104–106.

**Physical distraction** All meditation sittings involve a stage where the everyday mind tries to assert itself. This manifests in an increase in mental activity or other forms of distraction such as an itch or the urge to cough or fidget. In the main, you overcome these by gently directing your attention back to your breathing.

Sometimes the discomfort is hard to ignore. If you are seated in a traditional floor position, aches and pains are never far away. There are two ways you can respond to these. The ideal is to treat them as something to be aware of, but not to react to. The other way is to forget martyrdom, change your position, then move on with your meditation.

Besides, the best results come when you're more curious about the sound of your breathing than you are about the distraction.


## For the next few weeks

Deep~By Numbers is all you need for the first few months of your practice. If you're impatient to continue, stay with this for at least a few weeks. Put 2+10+1 aside each day. Turn up. Then relax and enjoy what happens in each moment—without comparing it with any other, and without expecting anything from it. Enjoy it for the time and space it allows you.

If you get the urge to extend the period a little, say to 20 minutes, great. But if you're new to meditation, don't go past 30 minutes.

I should point out again that if you reach any stage in this book where you feel it's as far as you want to go, that's a good place to settle. A large proportion of the world's meditators use methods that are no more sophisticated than Deep~By Numbers.

As counting makes it much easier to remain focused, this is a good method to retain in your portfolio for those days when you just can't seem to get your mind into your practice. On such occasions, Deep~By Numbers is the perfect antidote to restiveness.

If you're new to meditation, put the book aside now and we'll resume the journey in a couple of weeks.

# Deep~Core

Ah, you're back.

Feeling more refreshed? It's time to explore the core skill of the Deep practices.

What makes this different from the previous practice is the Observe step. Here, instead of counting breaths, you just listen to the sound of your breathing.

CenterWidenListen *Take a couple of minutes to let go of the outside world: to Center, Widen, and Listen to the relaxed sound of your breathing.*

Observe *Observe the sound of each out breath in the moment that it occurs.*

*Listen as you breathe in and out, but focus on the outflow.*
*Keep listening for that sound—and no other—until there*
*is nothing else in your awareness. Really observe that one*
*sound. Hear each breath as if you were hearing it for the*
*first time.*

*No effort is required. And no comparison is possible.*
*What you're experiencing is all there is. This moment is*
*unique. Complete in every possible sense. So there's no*
*waiting for more information or understanding, you just*
*relish what unfolds as it unfolds.*

*Thoughts will arise from time to time. When you*
*become aware of them, calmly turn your attention back to*
*your breathing.*

*Keep listening.*

*Soon you'll be absorbed by the sound. Soon nothing else*
*will exist.*

*When the time is up, wait a minute or so before*
*moving. Don't try to evaluate what happened, just enjoy the*
*relaxed feeling.*

Stick with this version of Deep for the next few weeks. Stay longer if it feels right.

If you find you have difficulty keeping distraction at bay, spend the first few minutes counting the breath.

Most meditators who use concentrative approaches are happy to remain at this level. Maybe you will be, too. There's no hurry. Make your choice when the time's right. For the time being, all that matters is that you feel relaxed and comfortable with what you've learned so far. Besides, until you are really familiar with the practices, the difference between Deep~Core and other versions ahead is subtle.

# Deep~PoV

If you've been keeping your expectations in check, and you are just taking things as they come, you'll be feeling more comfortable with the Deep process by now.

The hardest part is simply resisting the urge to analyze what has been happening, or to compare it with what you think should be happening.

Around this stage you may start to notice subtle shifts in outlook beginning to occur. These will be very subtle. Possibly only slight improvements in mood, restfulness, and the ability to concentrate. If you are unaware of these yet, don't give it another thought. You have all the time in the world.

In previous Deep versions you were aware only of the "object," the sound of your breathing. Now we're going to add the subject to the mix: an awareness of who's doing the listening. Deep~PoV (Point of View) is about your perspective as a meditator.

When you turn your attention to who is reading this page, who comes to mind? Pause and think about it for a moment.

The obvious answer is "I am." But if you keep pondering this, you may come to the question, where am "I" located? Am I my body? Am I my heart? My legs? My eyes? My brain? My body–mind? For now, let's settle on a place from which you might be able to imagine the "I" thought originates.

In some Eastern traditions, the self is said to reside in a place known as the third eye. This is located in the center of your forehead, slightly behind the eyebrows. In Tantra, this is the location of the sixth or brow *chakra*, which relates to higher intuition, psychic abilities, spiritual connection, holistic view, and the capacity to transcend the ego or earthly identity. René Descartes called this "the seat of the soul," and believed it was related to the pineal gland, which classically was said to be the organ of spiritual perception, intuition, and the connection between physical and spiritual worlds. (The pineal gland is a bit out of the way and not all that relevant, in my opinion.)

There is a more compelling reason why the center-of-the-forehead position works so well as the focus of your meditation, and as the imaginary location of I.

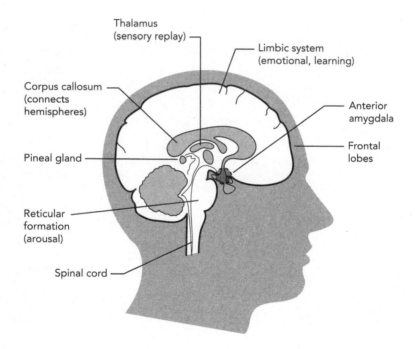

The center of your forehead aligns with the *anterior amygdala*, an almond-shaped neural structure in the temporal lobe of your brain—directly behind your eyebrows.

The anterior amygdala is associated with creativity, motivation, insight, intelligence, and pleasure. When stimulated, it can produce instantaneous and sometimes dramatic increases in your levels of creativity, intelligence, and positive emotions. Such increases have been measured in laboratory experiments. Stimulation can also produce mystical or paranormal experiences.

More pertinent still, *you can produce this stimulation* yourself—not by using the minute electric currents that laboratories rely on, but through your own mental processes, such as meditation and guided imagery. The results of the latter have also been measured in some studies.

There's no need to sweat over the exact location of the anterior amygdala right now. If you imagine directing your attention from an area somewhere behind the eyebrows, you can produce the effect.

You may find it easier if you imagine seeing what you're seeing *from behind your eyes*, rather than through them. Similarly, try to imagine *hearing from inside your head*, rather than through your ears.

Try it now.

If you prefer, you can approach this experiment from an entirely 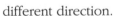 different direction.

Close your eyes, then allow them to drift upward—as if you were looking at a point 40 inches or so in front of you, say 20 to 40 degrees above the horizon. There will be one particular angle where your eyes feel relaxed and natural.

With that sensation in mind, imagine your attention is being directed from just behind your eyebrows.

Imagine it now.

**CenterWidenListen** *Take a couple of minutes to let go of the outside world: to Center, Widen, and Listen to the relaxed sound of your breathing.*

**Observe** *Observe the sound of each breath—as if you are hearing it from the place where "I" is located.*

*Even though you are aware of who is meditating, observe only the sound of each breath. You can imagine hearing this from inside your head, rather than through your ears.*

*There is no room in your consciousness for what's going to happen, or what should be happening, because you are in the center of it all. There are no thoughts about what you're experiencing, you just experience it. Just the sound. And you keep listening until the separation between the listener and the sound dissolves. Now there is no sense of self, only a sense of sound.*

Some people find Deep~PoV helps them to feel more centered. However, it is a way of using the imagination that doesn't appeal to all people. If it doesn't grab you, just move on.

# Deep~Visual

Most adults favor one sense over another in the way they interpret life and respond to language. I don't know if you've noticed this or not, but there are subtle appeals to each of your senses in the methods I've included so far. You may have thought I was favoring the sense of hearing—"*Listen* to your breathing," "*Listen* to a distant *sound*"—but this is an illusion. The central sensation in this book relates to breathing: not a sound, but a feeling. I've also been writing about the *object* of your meditation, and *focusing* your attention on it. Focusing and objects relate to visual activities, right? The fact that the object of your focus is a sound that you feel is my way of overcoming all the unknown sensory biases you may have. There is a sound reason for this that will become much clearer when you go on to Book B.

Now we're going to look at how the visual sense can be better utilized on some occasions.

Deep~Visual is for those times you'd like to add more spiritual flavor or atmosphere to your meditation. It's also for when you have a resistance to using your other senses for some reason or another. Such as when you have a head cold or a sniffle and don't wish to focus on your breathing. It may also come in handy if you ever need some extra "horsepower" to get your mind off a particular topic.

Instead of struggling or missing out on your practice altogether, you simply substitute something visual as the object of your attention.

The first thing is to decide what this "something visual" is. Many meditation schools base their practices around an image or physical object. These vary from the meaningless (a candle flame) to the meaningful (a sacred image) to the fantastic (a mental image) to the abstract (a mandala).

If you have a strong religious belief, an image has probably already sprung to mind. Now the key to connecting your meditation to your spiritual practice is just to add this visual element.

The alternative is to choose something mesmerizing such as a candle flame. Once you've decided on the object, the rest of the process should be familiar.

**CenterWidenListen** *Take a couple of minutes to let go of the outside world: to Center, Widen, and Listen to the relaxed sound of your breathing.*

**Observe** *Closely observe the image or object in front of you, without seeking any meaning from it.*

*Either with your eyes closed or half open, direct your attention toward that object or image. Be aware of nothing else. If your eyes are half open, take care to keep your vision soft and relaxed. Avoid staring, as you'll be distracted by watery eyes. It's okay to blink in the usual way.*

*Observe only the object. Not what it means, or how it has been manufactured, or its aesthetics. Just observe the object in one moment.*

*When random thoughts arise, bring your attention back to the visual. Not for what it means, or for how it looks. Just observe, without judgment or analysis.*

*Soon your attention will be filled with the image, and that alone.*

## It was deeper than you thought

After some sittings you may come to the conclusion that all you did during the time was churn ideas. "I suddenly became aware that after long periods of sitting there, I wasn't meditating at all—I was daydreaming." In your mind you'd been entertaining a long stream of thoughts, with little or no meditation involved.

Sometimes this is what happens. It doesn't matter in the slightest. In time, though, you'll recognize it as a trick of the rational mind. An illusion.

You believe this is what happens because in some meditative states the Beta and Alpha brain-wave frequencies (those that relate to everyday awareness) are suppressed. When this occurs, there's little recollection of what took place during that phase. You remember the bits that occurred when you were thinking or daydreaming, but have no recollection of the rest. In some ways this is like when you wake from a "long" dream that you're convinced has been going on all night. Then you check the clock and realize you've only been asleep a few minutes.

In deep meditative states, as in the dream state, time does not exist. At least not in the sense that you normally experience it. When you look back on the experience, you tend to remember the distracting elements rather than the more subtle ones. Or you remember the thoughts or the dreams, but not the meditation or the sleep.

# The role of Deep

Each of the Quiet practices leads to the material and spiritual benefits that we covered earlier in this book. The Deep practices play a unique role in this. Primarily, they help to remove the clutter and limitations of everyday awareness so you can become intuitively aware of life's big picture. When the mind is still, this occurs quite spontaneously—without the filtration of conscious thought.

The principle is exquisitely simple. You observe the object of your meditation until there is no longer any separation between you and the object. The more often you do this, the more you begin to intuit the unity of all things.

The Deep practices also share a subsidiary advantage that many see as their main benefit: they produce a beautiful state of tranquility, more so than the other approaches. This is why some traditions refer to concentrative methods as "serenity meditation." Over time the Deep practices transform this into a level of inner calm that stays with you permanently.

You can do what millions of meditators do and use Deep practices exclusively; or you can do what I do, and use them in conjunction with other Quiet practices. In this way, Deep becomes a powerful way of enhancing your concentrative abilities, which in turn makes it easier for you to use the Aware methods in the pages ahead.

Whatever approach you finally settle on, keep the Deep practices as part of your portfolio, especially Deep~By Numbers. It's simple and foolproof, and is ideal for those restless patches in your life or practice.

| QUIET PRACTICE 1 | | |
|---|---|---|
| DEEP | By Numbers | Counting breaths |
| | Core | Focusing on breath |
| | PoV | Adding point of view |
| | Visual | A visual element as a point of focus |

# QUIET PRACTICE 2: DIRECTED

A few years ago I was at a business function where a 90-year-old Indian *yogini* was about to speak. She looked at the microphone for a moment, then invited everyone to join her in meditation. One of her aides looked about the room, correctly assumed that the audience consisted mostly of nonmeditators, then whispered: "Dadi, perhaps we should explain the method of meditation first."

"There's no need for method," she said, and laughed. "All we have to do is sit and be with God."

It was a pivotal moment for those who felt they had a relationship with God. They instantly knew what her meditation was about.

The Directed practices are for when you have a clear idea of where you'd like your spiritual practice to take you. In one sense it's like the contemplative practices in religions such as Christianity and

Islam, and some aspects of Hinduism. In another sense it's a way of exploring spiritual themes or concepts in order to discover the deeper truths behind them.

Directed has a special appeal to followers of Western religions, which tend to emphasize the verbal over the experiential. If you have such a leaning or background, you may find additional comfort in such a thoughtful, word-based approach.

The fact that it involves thought doesn't mean it's more cerebral than other Quiet practices. In a Directed sitting your thoughts are the vehicle that helps you to focus. The more they fill your attention, the closer you are to one-pointedness.

Rather than being a discursive or analytical process, or a series of random thoughts where you can distract yourself with whatever comes along, this approach employs an intentional line of thinking that leaves no room for *unwanted* thought. In other words, Directed is a concentrative type of meditation like Deep.

Both approaches have an "object" in mind, but where Deep allows room only for the object, Directed allows a stream of thoughts that lead you to it.

Your intent and the choice of object are what give Directed its spiritual relevance. Your intent might be to have a closer relationship with the Supreme, so the object would be the Supreme. Your intent might be to radiate loving-kindness toward a group of people you know, so your object would be those people. If your intent was to imbibe the deeper meaning of scriptures, your object might be God or oneness.

Each of these intents involves an end point. By directing your attention toward this, without distraction or digression, you achieve a state where you and the object of your meditation form some sort of union—at least insofar as your attention is concerned.

Not only does this produce the meditative state we've covered before but it colors it according to your particular interest. So if you approach a Directed sitting from a Christian perspective, you'll feel you are having a Christian-type experience. If you feel deeply about your religion or your personal relationship with the Supreme, you will bring a sense of reverence to your meditation. If you're moved by a sense of compassion toward all others, you will bring love to it. Or if you can see through the illusions of ego, you will bring a sense of selflessness.

So in this sense, Directed can be part of, or an extension of, your spiritual practice.

The flavor or preconditioning that you start out with is integral to it.

Usually this will involve a powerful emotion such as reverence or love, which an electroencephalogram (EEG) shows can produce a similar mental state to meditation.

The thoughts you employ can be a sequence of linked concepts or just a few simple phrases that you revisit over and over—just like a mantra with meaning. After some time of this, individual thoughts begin to dissolve and, probably without you being aware of any change whatsoever, your attention will be communing with the object of your meditation.

But before you put this into a working perspective, there are two questions you need to resolve: where you want to end up, and what line of thoughts will take you there.

Unlike the former Quiet practices, Directed has an intention. Technically, an intention is not the same as a goal, but it does point you in a specific direction. To be effective, it should dovetail with whatever spiritual journey you're on.

Here are a few examples:

- *"My intention is to share the peace and harmony I experience in meditation with all sentient beings."*
- *"My intention is to experience a sense of oneness with all things."*
- *"My intention is to know God and experience the joy of being in His company."*
- *"My intention is to enable my soul to act like a mirror to the universal self."*
- *"My intention is to establish a one-on-one communication with the Supreme."*
- *"My intention is to see through the illusion of the self, and come face-to-face with that which is real."*

Once you've decided where you want to end up, you can decide what line of thoughts will lead you there.

This line can be either formal or informal. If formal, you'll start with a predefined set of words. If informal, you'll start with a concept or a formula.

There are many traditions that view contemplation as an exercise where you intellectualize your way around a theme or passage until you arrive at some deeper meaning. Because this locks you into an everyday state of consciousness, it is different in intent from the Directed practices.

Directed uses the words or thoughts as a way of changing your state so that you can *intuitively* understand something better. It's a subtle, but vital difference. Intellectualization, or foraging around in search of deeper meaning, actually impedes your meditation. Whereas neutrally observing the thoughts or words from a meditative state—without analysis or revision—produces an intuitive understanding that's much deeper.

With Directed you observe the words or sequence of thoughts in the moment that they come into your attention. Then you let them pass.

They come into and out of your field of attention like clouds going past your window. You appreciate them for the beauty of the moment. You derive what understanding there is to be derived, without pausing to review or think about it. There are no replays, no wondering what that last one really meant, no wondering what's going to come next—just total acceptance and observation of all that is before you in this moment.

That is when the most profound understandings arise.

# The formal approach

The formal line of thought can range from traditional prayers, to passages from the scriptures, to mantras, to composed meditations.

If it's spiritual significance you're after, it would be best to make your choice from the tradition or teaching you most relate to. The words you choose should be committed to memory or actually read from a *familiar* text.

An example of the latter is where the meditator slowly reads a section from the scriptures or some sacred text, carefully absorbing each sentence or verse—without revision—then pausing to allow it to reveal its meaning. Sometimes this might lead to spontaneous prayer.

In some schools, the actual learning of the words is a part of the process. In this case, precision is essential—not only in the words and phrases, but in pronunciation and even inflections— because the object is to gain mastery of the mind through focused attention.

But as you're the only person involved in the practice, it's up to you to decide what level of accuracy to aim for. My belief is that as long as you've memorized the general thrust of the words, to the extent that they flow freely and effortlessly, you've done all that's required.

The beauty of the formal approach is that the words you use may have historical or spiritual significance for you, over and above their actual meaning. This can have a powerful effect on the way you feel. The downside is that you become too concerned with their accuracy during your meditation, which works against what you're trying to achieve. Even with the best intentions you'll probably find that the words become more abstract as you near your intended destination.

Is Directed just another form of prayer? Some teachers say that prayer is speaking, whereas meditation is listening. Or in the words of one mystic, "In prayer I speak to God; in meditation God speaks to me." I think it's all a matter of intention. If both prayer and meditation can lead to a union with the divine, and that's your intention, who cares about the distinctions?

Advocates of mantra tend to fall into three camps: those who believe that the special vibrations of the words connect the individual mind with the universal mind; those who believe the words invoke the divine; and those who believe they are just sounds. Some claim a mantra must come from a guru or teacher, and others say you can get them from the Internet. Make your own choice.

I've included a range of formal examples on this book's website (www.evenmorequiet.com). These include sacred texts from different religions, mantra, even poetry.

Here's how to use them in a Directed session. To begin with, decide where you intend to end up. Then decide what set of words or thoughts is going to take you there.

CenterWidenListen  *Take a couple of minutes to let go of the outside world: to Center, Widen, and Listen to the relaxed sound of your breathing.*

Observe  *Observe the flow of thoughts or words that lead you toward the Supreme (for instance).*

*When you are deeply relaxed, start listening to the sound of your voice articulating the chosen words.*
   *Whether you do this aloud or in your imagination doesn't matter.*
   *Observe the sound of each word or phrase, being open to any meaning it might impart. At all times, be aware of the end destination—where the words or thoughts are taking you.*
   *After a while, the words or thoughts become almost transparent, and your attention will be filled with the goal of your meditation.*

## When someone else calls the shots

The most obvious version of the formal approach is guided meditation. Here someone else assumes responsibility for the content, and guides you through the various steps.

When done skillfully, this can be a powerful way to begin an involvement with the Quiet practices. But I would suggest that this is for the early days only, and you'd be better served taking responsibility for your own practice.

# The informal approach

The informal route is more freewheeling. Here, instead of having a set of formally defined words to learn and remember, you have an outline. Or a road map. The only discipline involved is sticking to that map to the best of your abilities, while you allow your thoughts to take you where they will. Remember, the map is just a guide; it's not meant to be a test of concentration.

As a demonstration, examine the structure of this Buddhist **Loving-kindness** meditation or *metta*. On first viewing, it may appear a little forced, but in practice it is a powerful way to share with others the peacefulness you are developing within yourself.

As simple as it is, Loving-kindness is quite an advanced meditation for people who are completely at peace within themselves. There is a caveat: if you attempt it before you are ready, you'll struggle to get past the first step. But it's worth persevering to get past that first step.

Loving-kindness begins with you being able to fully accept yourself in a loving way. Once you've done this, you are ready to "spread" this compassionate feeling, step by step, toward others—starting with someone you have loving feelings for, then progressively working your way through a list of people until you come to your enemies, and then to all sentient beings.

So your list of people to "radiate" Loving-kindness to might include:

- yourself
- a lover or partner
- someone close to you, such as a family member
- an admired and respected figure

- an acquaintance whom you have no specific feelings about
- an enemy, or someone you have poor relations with
- all sentient beings.

Choose whatever words you like to express this, but the *sentiment* behind each stage of your meditation will be along the lines of: "May I be filled with loving-kindness. May I be happy and peaceful, and live with ease."

In spite of the way it's structured here, this isn't a prayer or a request for some kind of external intervention. Loving-kindness is an outward-focused exercise intended to enhance your ability to love, and to radiate positive, loving energy toward others. It has the additional benefit of helping you rebuild the bonds with somebody else—dissolving problems and barriers without expecting the other person to change.

Some teachers encourage you to "sense" this loving feeling in your breast area (aligning with the heart *chakra*, which is considered to be the center for spiritual healing, and the channel for universal love). It's also where people sense the feeling of love.

First decide where you intend to end up. Then start the following exercise.

CenterWidenListen *Take a couple of minutes to let go of the outside world: to Center, Widen, and Listen to the relaxed sound of your breathing.*

Observe *Observe the feeling of love that you radiate from the core of your being.*

*When you're deeply relaxed, imagine hearing the sound
of your voice articulating words along the lines of the
following:*

- *May I be filled with loving-kindness. May I be happy
  and peaceful, and live with ease.*
- *May Tania [example] be filled with loving-kindness.
  May she be happy and peaceful, and live with ease.*
- *May Dr. Watson [example] be filled with loving-kindness.
  May he be happy and peaceful, and live with ease.*

And so on.

As each set of words enters your mind, feel yourself radiating a warm and loving feeling to the party it refers to. Continue through the list, repeating each set of words, until there are no words—only compassion, radiating boundlessly in all directions, to all people, to all beings.

Hold on to this energy as long as you can. Take it with you as you return to the wider world.

## A point of light

Light plays a big role in meditation folklore. Some meditators talk about experiencing it in one form or another in almost a thrill-seeking sort of way. Some Tantric practices focus on different-colored lights for different *chakras*. And shamans since the beginning of time have endowed light with mysterious qualities and meanings.

My interest is in its relationship to spiritual experience.

Throughout history, meditators and mystics have made references to brilliant light, or a point of light, or divine light, as a way of bringing the subtlety of their experiences into the physical realm. For the millions who have enjoyed transcendent levels of consciousness in meditation, such expressions seem somehow familiar.

The enlightened ones of all traditions are familiar with the clear, white light of self-realization or God-realization. Yoga tradition sometimes refers to a bright dot, or a distant point of light called a *bindu*. In metaphysical terms this is like the point where all phenomena converge—where space and time cease, where the past and future do not exist, where the intellect is transcended, and where Absolute Reality is experienced. (Another explanation is that the *bindu* represents the infinite silence that the *aum* mantra takes you to. In this case, it's metaphorically similar to the Quiet.)

The mystics of religions such as Christianity or Islam would be more inclined to equate any point of light with the Supreme. Certainly there have been many reports over the ages of witnessing "a being of light."

If you were to marry all of the above views, you might equate that light with the point of creation. Of infinity. Of the eternal.

For the moment, let's assume that all of these are metaphors. In worldly terms, seeing a point of light in meditation is akin to seeing light at the end of a tunnel. If you have time to imagine during your meditation, you can make your way along this tunnel (metaphorically speaking) until you reach the source. Then you are witnessing the clear white light of pure consciousness.

To place this into a more accessible context, we can cite the experiences of some meditators who report the sensation of light— say a pinpoint of brilliance—in the forehead area, somewhere between the eyebrows. There are a number of neurological theories as to why this occurs, but it works just as powerfully as a feature of the imagination.

Here's how to use an imaginary point of light—perhaps as a representation of the Supreme, or the Absolute Reality—as the object of your meditation.

First, decide what that point of light represents. Then, enjoy the following exercise.

CenterWidenListen *Take a couple of minutes to let go of the outside world: to Center, Widen, and Listen to the relaxed sound of your breathing.*

Observe *Observe an imaginary point of light in front of you, as a stream of thoughts leads toward it.*

*With this point of light firmly in mind, let your mind fill what stands between you and the object of your meditation.*

*This stream of thoughts will most likely be sparse and unstructured, and probably not worded as follows, but it will always be directing you to this one point.*

- *I am a being of light. My nature is light. My attention is focused on a tiny point of light in the center of my forehead.*
- *From this point of consciousness I radiate a stream of loving energy beyond this physical body. Toward an imaginary point of light in the distance. The farther it reaches, the freer and lighter I feel.*
- *As I feel myself coming closer to this light, I'm aware that I am coming closer to the serene, loving radiance of the Supreme.*
- *Now I realize that I am not just a point of light, but an integral part of that divine radiance.*

Obviously there's a distinct philosophical point of view in that thought stream. There's no need for you to follow it, of course. Feel free to substitute any viewpoint you feel comfortable with.

# Beyond 20 minutes

If everything has been progressing smoothly to this point, you might like to try extending your sitting to 30 minutes. Maybe even twice a day. It's not essential, but will deepen your practice.

If you're leading a busy, active life, an hour out of your day may seem like quite a chunk. You might think that finding this time means you have to rearrange your day or forgo certain activities. As for the suggestion that you might wake an hour earlier—you're not getting enough sleep as it is, so *anything* but that! However, one of the delightful surprises of the Quiet practices is that as they become an integral part of your life, you discover an hour of practice more than compensates for an hour of lost sleep. At least it does for most people.

Once you realize this, rising an hour earlier is not only painless, it's desirable. I'm not exaggerating. You can't wait to rise and get into your meditation. You think of it as a treat. This usually leads to a reorientation of your attitudes toward rising. Even so-called night people find this happening—their focus starts to shift to the start of their day rather than the end. Every person is different, though, so you may have to find a more creative way of working with your schedule.

There's another reason why a time will come when you'll want to extend your sitting period. Experienced long-distance runners talk about a "runner's high," which is the euphoric state they experience at a certain phase of a run. Casual joggers miss out on this. Why? First, a certain degree of fitness is required. Second, it kicks in after you've been engaged in the activity for around 30 minutes. If you spend your life doing 20-minute jogs, you may get all the health benefits, but never get to experience the euphoria of the runner's high.

It's the same with meditation.

At a certain phase, there can be a noticeable change in mental state that you might describe as euphoric. Although this could happen at any stage for a long-term meditator, it would be unlikely to occur before the 30-minute mark for someone less experienced. So if you were to spend your whole life doing short sittings (say, 2+10+1), you'd still get the physical and psychological benefits, but may never get to experience the euphoria that *sometimes* comes from longer sittings.

Be open to the possibility of extending your Quiet sittings from 2+10+1 to 20 minutes and, when the time is right, to 30 minutes. In months to come you can extend this even further if you wish. But there's no hurry; you have all the time in the world.

Finally, in using powerfully emotive words like "euphoria," I run the risk of raising expectations. This can be doubly disadvantageous: first, because even long-term meditators don't experience stuff like this every time they meditate; and second, because if you expect something to happen in meditation, it's usually a strong indication that it won't.

Only when you let go of expectation can things progress.

# The role of Directed

When you have a clear idea of where you'd like your spiritual pursuits to take you, use the formal or informal Directed practices.

If you belong to an established religion or faith, there can be great comfort in having a structured practice that aligns with your beliefs and understandings. Whether structured or unstructured, Directed provides the framework to pursue these.

It also sits comfortably with almost all spiritual traditions, especially those that have a contemplative component.

However, the Directed practices are not limited to faith-based activities. For example, there can be immense spiritual power that flows from bringing supercharged feelings such as reverence and compassion to your practice—as you saw with the Loving-kindness meditation—regardless of the beliefs you might have.

And when you're ready for it, Directed practices can also be used as a testing ground for these beliefs.

| QUIET PRACTICE 2 | | |
|---|---|---|
| DIRECTED | Formal | Using words from scripture, etc. |
| | Loving-kindness | Radiating a feeling of love |
| | Point of light | Moving from self to divine object |

# QUIET PRACTICE 3:  AWARE

Now we come to a significant departure from the previous Quiet practices. Where they served to concentrate your attention on only one thing or a series of things, Aware broadens it so that you are aware of many or all things simultaneously.

In one sense, these two approaches are virtual opposites: the concentrative styles (Deep and Directed) narrow your attention, the mindful style widens it; the former ignores the distractions that arise, the latter observes them.

Ultimately, though, both approaches achieve the same result: they help you bypass uninvited thought so your awareness remains pure and unobstructed.

The Aware practices take this one step further. They're designed to bring moment-to-moment awareness to all aspects of your life—not just to meditation.

They do this by training their attention to remain in the present.

Few people in today's world have this ability. They spend their life being aware only of what's already gone. Past tense. When you think, *I really like this flavor; I wonder if it's lemon or lime*, you are not involved in the present experience of taste, you are evaluating something that's already happened.

Of course, it's not always like this. There are moments when you're fully engaged in the present. Like when you're doing something physical, or when you lose yourself in an activity and totally forget about the rest of the world. Or in the instant you become aware of something, but haven't yet categorized what it is: the burst of laughter from the person sitting next to you on the bus, for example. This is a moment of pure, unconditioned awareness.

Aware practice trains you to extend that moment.

If you can be coolly aware of what's going on as it happens—without interfering or getting involved—something very revealing takes place. You are not only more aware of the experience, you are more aware of *you*, and what makes you tick. You start to see into the true nature of your personality, emotions, moods, and reactions, and even physical states such as pleasure and pain.

You can probably see the psychological advantages in this. Say, for example, you were experiencing a negative state or emotion like fear. Generally, you'd do everything in your power to shift your attention away from fear. You try to avoid it by denying its existence or by "compensating" in some way. Distracting yourself with fantasies about what you'll be doing tomorrow, or dragging up memories about something that happened yesterday—anything but face what you're feeling right now.

This means you never get to explore the nature of your emotion and how you react to it.

Common sense says that if you're going to learn to live with fear (to continue the above example), you have to come to grips with the fact that you feel afraid sometimes.

Then you start to understand that fear does more than make you feel tense and apprehensive. If you try to banish it, you produce stress. If you try to resist it, or pretend it doesn't exist, it reemerges in unpredictable ways. And if you leave it unattended, it leads to other emotions. As Yoda said in *Star Wars*: "Fear leads to anger; anger leads to hate; hate leads to suffering."

If you can bring clarity and objectivity to your feelings, you can accept that what you're feeling is simply what you're feeling. And there's nothing inherently good, bad, defining, or blameworthy about that. In time you learn to accept that all feelings, attitudes, and experiences are transitory. Soon you begin to understand what is real and important, and what is not.

This was one of the lessons of my childhood experience in the outback. When you're in the middle of nowhere, enveloped by 122-degree heat, there's not a lot you can do to escape it. Even when there is a bit of shade under the mulga trees, you can't hide from 122 degrees. With no sign of a breeze, what would you do?

If you did what most people do, you'd fan yourself, loosen your clothing, remove unnecessary garments, and shift from one position to another trying to find relief. But this makes you feel the heat more. So you turn to the imagination. You try to distract yourself mentally, going back to the past or to something planned for the future, and struggle to take your mind off the heat. But there's no hiding from it.

Try to imagine what would happen if instead of turning away, you turned to what is here. Instead of trying to distract yourself, you explore the nature of what's happening in this moment—in this instance, the heat.

And you're open to your reaction to it. You place yourself in the center of the heat experience, and observe without obstruction. A remarkable thing happens. You discover that it's not heat that causes you distress, it's how you respond to it. And when you coolly observe your responses rather than the event that produces them, both lose their sting.

The Aware practices place you in the center of every experience, so that you can observe them with clarity.

In this way it's similar to Buddhism's insight or *vipassana* practice, which teaches mindfulness in all facets of life. Among other things, this makes you aware of the changing nature of everything around you. Not only is this an elegant way of dealing with experiences like being too hot, it systematically removes the angst that usually goes with change, loss, aging, and death.

> Aware practices enable you to be in the very center of what you experience, and to observe it with complete clarity.
>
> This leads to a state of equanimity you can maintain no matter what is going on around you.

# The practice

Even though our initial focus is on the meditation sitting, the Aware practices go much further. They are the basis of a whole-of-life practice called Ongoing that we'll be covering later (see page 155).

In some ways, Aware is similar to the practices we have already covered, Deep and Directed:

- You put aside 20–30 minutes (or as little as 2+10+1 if you're pressed for time).
- You use a chair, meditation bench, cushion, or any of the floor positions.
- Your eyes are closed or slightly open.
- You do it without effort, analysis, or expectation.

Now the differences:

- Your focus is inclusive rather than exclusive. For example, where Deep focused on the outflow breath, Aware attends to the total act of breathing.
- Instead of trying to circumvent "distractions" that arise, you observe them neutrally—without involvement, engagement, or ownership.
- There is a perceived difference in your level of alertness. (Ideally there will be no difference, but it will seem as though there is.)

One of the drawbacks of attempting to be aware of many things simultaneously is that it invites distraction. This is why the Aware practice involves a rallying point, an anchoring observation. Then, when your attention strays, you know where to bring it back to.

In all cases, we use the breath as that rallying point.

From that point on, the Aware practices explore the nature of your life from several different viewpoints, in each instance bringing all of your attention to what you're experiencing at that moment.

The three main areas of exploration are the areas you're most intimate with: your body, your emotions, and your mind. You explore these separately, and collectively.

**Awareness of the physical body** traditionally involves a range of practices that start with the breath, then postures (walking, standing, sitting, etc.), daily action (work, exercise, etc.), and parts of the body, as well as some really strange stuff we won't be going into here. Our practices focus on breathing and parts of the body.

**Awareness of feelings and emotions** involves the observation of emotions as they well up and pass—without judgment or analysis.

**Awareness of states of mind** is similar to emotions, but is more concerned with general states: peaceful, loving, restless, and so on. The object is simply to be aware that these states arise and pass, without trying to manipulate them in any way.

We'll explore these three areas in separate practices. When you're more familiar with them, you might choose to combine the practices in a single sitting.

## OBSERVING WITHOUT THINKING

The object of the Aware practices is to produce pure, uncluttered awareness of what is.

Because awareness only exists in the present, you must be fully aware of what you're experiencing in the moment that it happens.

You can identify this experience, you can even name it if you like, but the moment you pause to think or analyze, you've moved the experience into the past.

Observe without evaluation or judgment.

# Aware~Breath

Our intention here is to use the movement of the breath to keep your awareness in the present. You do this by being in the center of the breathing, and observing it with fascination.

Being "in the center" relates to your perspective: as if the experience was taking place all around you. Now, by applying your full attention to the total act of breathing, you can coolly observe the centerpiece of your physical existence: the breath.

The object is to observe the physical sensations as they change from one moment to the next. As one breath is replaced by another breath, as cool inflow becomes warm outflow, and so on.

In doing this, you may be aware of how you respond to your breathing, but you won't try to modify or influence this response in any way. Just assume the role of the passive observer.

There are many ways to do this, but the simplest focuses your attention on where the air enters and leaves your nostrils or mouth.

> *Take a deep breath now. Feel the cool air flow somewhere near the edges of your nostrils or lips. This may be subtle, but there will be a distinct temperature change and sensation at this point. Do this a few times until it's clear in your mind. Remember this point.*
>
> *Next, breathe out heavily. Depending on whether you breathe out through your nose or your mouth, you'll feel a warmer airflow at your nostrils or lips.*

For the duration of your sitting, your attention will be centered around these two points.

CenterWidenListen  *Take a couple of minutes to let go of the outside world: to Center, Widen, and Listen to the relaxed sound of your breathing.*

Observe  *Observe the sensation of breathing in the moment that it occurs.*

*With eyes open or closed, your gaze softly focused just slightly in front of your nose, move your attention away from what you are hearing to what you are feeling—the physical sensation of breathing.*

*Be fully aware of the movement of air at your nostrils or lips. Feel the cool inflow of air as you inhale.*

*Then, as you breathe out, be fully aware of the movement of air at your nostrils or lips. If you've trained yourself to hear the sound of your out-breath in previous Quiet practices, you may still hear it. This doesn't matter; just keep your attention on the* sensation *of breath.*

*Continue to breathe this way—noting the sensation of the leisurely inflow and outflow as they occur at their own pace.*

*After many minutes of this you may notice that there is a tiny pause between the inflow and the outflow. Rather than being a continuous in-out action, you actually experience an instant of no breath. Observe that moment as well as the sensation that precedes and follows it.*

*As the sitting progresses, and you relax even more, your breath becomes subtle and light. You may lose track of it*

*altogether. When this happens, just return your attention
to the entry and exit points, and you'll see that those subtle
sensations are still present.*

*Feel the sensation of air as it passes the entry point.
Then wait for the sensation as it passes the exit point. Only
those two points.*

*And that's all you have to do.*

Of course, if any of the above steps cause psychological distress, just move on and use one of the other practices in this book. You can always come back to this practice one day in the future.

## An addition you can count on

In introducing you to Aware, I've made the assumption that you've been applying the various Quiet practices as you've been reading about them. Having done so, you'll find the transition from the concentrative practices to Aware is a comfortable step.

This won't be the case for everyone. I recall that my introduction to awareness practice at 16 or so was a confusing and restless period—not at all what I expected from meditation. (See what happens when you have expectations?)

If you struggle with the practice as I've described it above, you can make it more accessible by adding a few simple words.

Observe  *Observe the sensation of breathing, and count each
breath in the moment that it occurs.*

*The idea is to use counting to keep you on track, just as you did with the first version of Deep.*

*The main difference here is that you are focused on the sensation of breathing, the in-breath as much as the out-breath. When you breathe in, you hear the quietest count of "one." And when you breathe out, you also hear the count of "one."*

*Breathe in, "two." Breathe out, "two." And so on. When you get to 10, restart the count.*

Even though it is used the world over, counting can be a fairly blunt instrument when it comes to the Aware practices. It can be useful when you're feeling distracted, restless, or under pressure, but there are more elegant methods for your ongoing practice.

A popular alternative is a process known as naming. As you breathe in, you hear a subtle voice saying "Breathing in." As you breathe out, you hear it saying "Breathing out." This makes a clear distinction between one action and another, so you become even more aware of your breathing, especially as your sitting progresses and the breath becomes subtle.

*Keep in mind here that you are attending to the act of breathing. As far as your attention is concerned, the words barely exist. You could think of them more like sighs than words. They have no purpose other than to keep you in touch with the subtle movements of your breath.*

*Keep hearing "breathing in" and "breathing out" for the duration of your sitting.*

*As basic as it seems, this is the foundation of a wider and more revealing practice. Breathing in and breathing out are just the beginning phases of a series of observations that reveal more and more about the total act of breathing.*

*Now you can broaden your field of attention to include the expansion of your rib cage, the extension of your diaphragm, and the overall movement of your upper body.*

Observe. *Observe the different components of the breathing action, and name each one as it occurs.*

*Start by being aware of the flow of air at your nostrils or lips. Maybe you can already hear the faint words "breathing in" "breathing out." Very faintly. Your attention is on breathing, not the names.*

*After a couple of minutes of this, broaden your attention to be aware of how breathing influences other parts of the body. In particular, pay attention to the rise and fall, contraction and expansion of your abdomen.*

*To begin with, you may notice the flow of warm air into your body. As the air flows into your lungs, be aware of the warmth and the movement. You might hear the subtle words "Flowing in" as this happens, and "Flowing out" as you breathe out.*

*After a period of this, follow the breath farther. You breathe in and your abdomen expands: be*

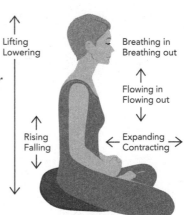

Lifting
Lowering

Rising
Falling

Breathing in
Breathing out

Flowing in
Flowing out

Expanding
Contracting

*aware of this physical movement and what it feels like. You
breathe out and it contracts: be aware of the movement and
sensation. As you do this, you might hear "Expanding" as
you breathe in, and "Contracting" as you breathe out.*

*After you have done this a number of times, slowly
become aware of the movement of air inside your lungs.*

*Breathing low into your lungs creates the sensation of
air being forced upward—so be aware of an upward force
as you breathe in. Note the rising sensation inside your
lungs. Then the falling sensation as the air is exhaled. Hear
"Rising" as you breathe in, and "Falling" as you breathe out.*

*After you've done this a number of times, let your
awareness take in the weight of your upper body. As you
breathe in, you'll note how it seems to lift slightly, bringing
a subtle sensation of lightness. As you breathe out, you'll feel
it lower, and the weight return. Hear "Lifting" as you breathe
in, and hear "Lowering" as you breathe out.*

*After you've done this a few times, be aware of the whole
of your upper body. As you breathe in, sense the lift and
expansion. As you breathe out, sense the fall and contraction.
Hear the words if it helps; ignore them if you prefer.*

So you can see the process here. It's bringing your awareness to your
entire physical body, bit by bit, through the vehicle of breathing.


## What do you think?

It is the nature of all meditation practices to be interrupted by
uninvited thought. Often when you've directed your awareness to
the subtle movements of your breath you start to lose touch with the

inflow and the outflow and, before you know it, you're compiling a shopping list.

Overcoming this involves another paradox. If you are attending to your breathing, there will be no thought; if thoughts arise, it means you are not attending to your breathing. Simple enough. But attending to the breathing is not meant to be a way of banishing thought—the breath is meant to be the link between body and mind, not the barrier.

The art is to recognize thoughts as part of the meditation process. They appear and they pass. When one appears, passively observe it—*Hmm, there's a thought*—and allow it to pass. Just like people walking past your open window, or an image floating past on a television screen. Passive observation. Without ownership, interest, or involvement. It's only when you *engage* a thought—when you get mentally involved in it in some way—that it becomes an impediment. Treat it with cool indifference.

When the thought passes, gently return your attention to your breathing.

Don't expect all this to happen in the first few weeks. It takes considerable practice to be able to remain neutral like this, but there are many rewards that flow from persistence. Not just the spiritual rewards that relate to nonattachment and recognizing impermanence, but the psychological ones that come from realizing you are not your thoughts, and that this moment is the only one that exists.

## How you'll feel

This is a small but vital point about the mental state associated with the Aware practice. In the early days of developing your meditation skills—particularly when you're using any of the Deep practices—you sometimes arrive at a very seductive, almost "glassy" state of restfulness that is only an eyelid flutter away from sleep.

When this occurs, you're not really conscious of much other than how pleasant it feels. All this means is that there's less prominence of Alpha and Beta, the brain frequencies we associate with everyday awareness.

The Aware practices strive to maintain a state that is slightly different from this. With Aware, your body and mind are in a deeply peaceful state, but you are always fully aware of what's going on. (This is also what you experience when you become proficient in the Deep practices.)

You may think this is not something you can consciously control, but it is. If you become aware of any sinking or lethargic feeling, just bring your attention back to the cool inflow of air at your nostrils or lips. Usually that's all it takes to restore full awareness.

If you still feel drowsy, here's a simple Yoga wake-up method that won't interrupt your meditation. Concentrate on the air flowing in through your right nostril, then flowing out through your left nostril. Then in through the left, out through the right. Continue this until you feel alert again.

## The breath as a constant

The object of each of the Aware practices is to be in the center of a particular aspect of your being—such as your breathing or what you're feeling. From this vantage point, you can observe it with fascination.

Because the breath is ever-present, always of the moment, and continually representative of the rising and passing of things, it is the constant between each of the Aware practices. So this means you can be in the center of "breathing" at the same time that you are in the center of "feeling," for example.

So no matter what the content of your awareness, you remain in the center of breathing at the same time that you remain in the center of everything else.

# Aware~Body

After a few weeks of attending to your breathing, you can move on to what your other senses are experiencing.

The first one to add to the mix is your sense of touch. In some ways you're already conditioned to this being part of your Aware practice—it relates to what you were feeling in the breathing practice earlier.

Aware~Body moves your attention around the physical body. You can do this in a number of ways, so it pays to decide on the "map" before you start out.

The object is just to be aware of any sensations that occur in the body while you're meditating.

CenterWidenListen  *Take a couple of minutes to let go of the outside world: to Center, Widen, and Listen to the relaxed sound of your breathing.*

Observe  *Observe any physical sensation that forces itself into your attention.*

*First turn your attention to the physical sensation of breathing.*

*After some time of this, bring your attention to what you can feel. Be aware of where your skin incurs resistance. Start with where one hand touches the other. Be aware of the pressure, the sensation, the weight. Be completely open to this sensation. Maybe you've never felt the weight of one hand against another before.*

*Don't go looking for sensations, just be open to them when they force their way into your awareness. Maybe you notice where the insides of your arms fall against the side of your body. Be aware of that sensation.*

*Perhaps the next sensation to come into your awareness is where your buttocks touch the chair or the cushion. (These are all examples.) You might then notice the skin inside your clothes. The weight and sensation of one leg crossing another. The sensation of your foot inside your sock. And when you've worked your way to the foot, work your way back.*

*To make this even smoother, you can try naming the sensation. "Touching, touching." "Brushing, brushing." "Pressing, pressing." When you make a clear distinction between subtle physical phenomena by applying a name to them, you'll find it easier to maintain awareness of the distinctions between them. This becomes particularly useful as your meditative state deepens, and things start to blend into one another.*

When you feel comfortable with this leisurely, unforced process, you can move on to a more expansive version that's based on a Southeast Asian Buddhist practice known as "sweeping."

Observe  *Observe any physical sensation that presents itself as
you move your focus from the top of your head to the bottom of
your feet.*

*The process is to move a narrow band of awareness over the
body, from head to toe.*

*You start at the place you are closest to now—the
physical sensation of breathing. Once your attention is filled
with this, you can begin to scan the body. Moving upward or
downward. The following are a few examples of how it could
go. It will vary according to what sensations bring themselves
to your attention.*

*Become aware of the feeling of your hair against
your ears. Make no assessments or comparisons about this
sensation, just be aware of it.*

*Next you might become aware of the saliva in your
mouth. As you move downward, you might be aware of the
temperature difference in the V of your shirt, or the dryness
in your throat. Don't look for the meaning in any of these,
just be aware of them as they appear.*

*Take your time. Continue, step by step, over the length of
your body: your collar against the nape of your neck, the weight
of your jacket on your shoulders, the itch on your hip, the
stiffness in your knee, the snugness inside your shoe, the fabric
of your sock against your toe. Then work your way back.*

*If it helps during this meditation, you can name each of
the sensations. "Tasting, tasting." "Stiffness, stiffness." "Touching,
touching."*

# Into pain and discomfort

It's possible to practice Aware~Body without strategy. Just sit and be aware of whatever comes up. Keep your attention on your breathing until such time as some kind of physical sensation makes its presence known. You won't be searching for distraction, nor particularly open to it, but sooner or later something will stick its head up. If or when this occurs just be aware of it.

Say, for example, your foot starts to ache while you're seated in meditation. There are three different ways you can deal with this: you can give in and change your position so the discomfort goes away; you can pretend it doesn't exist; or you can observe it with your full attention.

Your natural inclination is to react to it. To give in and change your posture may bring temporary relief, but it works against the intention of your meditation. So, instead, you try to distract yourself with thoughts. Once again, this compromises the meditation, and the discomfort resurfaces. In both cases, there's a flow-on effect: when you react to the discomfort, an emotion will flow from it—frustration, confusion, irritation, or even anger. This then leads to other reactions.

Sometimes it helps to name the sensation. "Pins and needles." "Backache." In this way you turn the discomfort into some kind of observable thing: it's not me, it's backache. And it's not backache that causes suffering, it's how you respond to it. Just observe. Maintain a bare, nonjudgmental awareness. And do your best not to respond to or get involved in the observation.

An attendee at one of my retreats told me how useful this ability can be. "I gave up coffee years ago because I wasn't sleeping well," she said. "Then, at a restaurant one evening, I agreed to a decaf at the end of dinner. I don't usually do this, as even a decaf disturbs my sleep. When this strong-tasting espresso arrived, I should have known. It was full strength. Guaranteed insomnia. But that night, as soon as I started to toss and turn, I remembered the Aware practices. Instead of fighting it, I placed myself in the center of my restlessness and just observed how it affected me and how I responded to it. You guessed it: I was asleep in minutes."

This counterintuitive approach works amazingly well for the experienced meditator. It hclps you to accept what is—even if it is painful or uncomfortable—without enhancing it with emotions like resentment, regret, denial, or frustration. Because it's often not the condition or the sensation that causes suffering, it's how you respond to it.

This can be a useful insight in the early days of Aware practice, when aches and pains always seem to turn up when you're most relaxed and peaceful. (There's a reason for this: the aches and pains are usually there during the day; you were just too distracted to notice.) If discomfort arises, observe it. Register the fact that discomfort is there, but apply no meaning or value to the observation. And if you do happen to react, then just observe that reaction as well—without applying meaning or value to it. The more impartial your observations, the stronger the mind becomes.

## A NOTE OF CAUTION

For the moment, please limit your efforts to minor discomforts. Don't try to use meditation as a way of dealing with acute pain, illness, or emotional conditions without the guidance of a teacher or a medical professional.

This same principle applies to severe or chronic pain. You accept that pain exists. Observing without judgment or avoidance may not diminish the discomfort, but it will help you avert those discomforts that flow from it, be they emotional or physical. Not surprisingly, the outcome of this may be that pain is reduced—in fact meditation techniques such as the above are frequently used in pain-control centers.

You can apply what you learn from the above practice to your other senses. Hearing is an obvious one, as you've been using it in the CenterWidenListen steps. Seeing is another. If you're interested in experimenting with these, check out this book's website.

# Aware~Feelings

Once you feel comfortable with the Aware approaches we've covered so far, you can advance to an area that is potentially more confrontational. Now you move away from the relatively safe area of your body and senses, and start exploring your emotions.

In some Eastern traditions, emotions are considered to be one of the six senses. You might think this makes more intuitive sense than the orthodox view that says emotions are activities of the mind.

Exploring what you are feeling has multiple benefits. It takes emotion out of the abstract, and makes it familiar. It helps to train the awareness to remain in the present. And it reveals that all feelings are transitory—they arise and they will pass—something you struggle to accept while you're being affected by them.

Aware~Feelings places you at the epicenter of everything you feel. This expands your capacity to embrace life. If you can experience your emotions fully—without trying to avoid or change them—you can open up to the full spectrum of human experience. This applies to negative as well as positive emotions. You discover that it's not that you experience a negative feeling that causes suffering, it's how you respond to it. And it's not that you experience a pleasurable feeling that causes attachment, it's whether you try to cling to it or not.

This can be complicated by the fact that we often have strange relationships with our emotions. We allow them to rule, confuse, deceive, bring shame or guilt, and guide our actions. We resent, deny, and even feel embarrassed about them. Yet being fully aware of them as they unfold brings acceptance and understanding.

While this is fairly simple in concept, it can be challenging in execution. It's simplified if you break the process down into three discrete stages.

The first is to **recognize** whatever is present. We're skilled at concealing or ignoring certain emotions, so they can often go unnoticed. When you really direct your attention toward what you're feeling, even the subtlest emotions can start to make their presence known.

Once you recognize an emotion, the next stage is to **name** it. This takes it out of the vague mental realm, and makes it more approachable. For example, "anger" is much easier to deal with than some unspecified nagging in your gut. Without trying to be precise with the terminology, calmly name what you are experiencing: "happiness," or "disappointment," or "love," or "impatience," or "jealousy."

The last stage is to **accept** it unconditionally. It is what it is. You don't get involved in it, or try to change, approve, or disapprove of it—you just accept it for what it is, and allow it to be. Without resisting or trying to hold on to it. An emotion has arisen because of a certain confluence of events, and it will pass.

In the context of a Quiet sitting, these three stages require complete openness. You can't manufacture the feelings, and you don't want to go searching for them. But if one arises and is compelling enough to claim your attention, recognize it, name it, and accept it.

CenterWidenListen *Take a couple of minutes to let go of the outside world: to Center, Widen, and Listen to the relaxed sound of your breathing.*

Observe  *Observe any emotion that arises in the moment that it occurs.*

*Just be aware of the breath. Even if it takes up the whole sitting, be aware of breathing.*

*Don't go searching for any particular feeling or emotion, but if one arises, and is compelling enough to claim your attention, let it fill your awareness.* Recognize *it.*

*Then* name *it: "Impatience, impatience." (There's no need to be precise. If you can't think of an appropriate name, just use "Feeling, feeling.")*

*Then* accept *it for what it is, rather than for what it means. In this way there's no attempt to resist, conceal, analyze, or respond to what you are experiencing. Just be in the center of it, and observe.*

*Observe how impatience manifests. The shuffling of the feet. The search for distraction. The urge to check your watch. Maintain your awareness of this—"Impatience, impatience"—until it passes.*

*Then, if another feeling follows, be aware of it.*
*Impatience might lead to a feeling of anger. Anger might*
*lead to regret. Regret might lead to love. Love might lead*
*to a feeling of pleasure. Without getting too involved in the*
*analysis, be aware of any associated stage. Pleasure has*
*arisen. "Pleasure, pleasure." Sometimes nothing follows at all,*
*and this can be noted as well.*

*If related thoughts arise and you find yourself*
*becoming involved in them, return to your breathing,*
*not to the emotion. Similarly, if you feel in any way*
*overwhelmed by what you are experiencing, just return*
*to breathing.*

Whether you follow the above steps in a formal sitting or in wider everyday life, they will help you to experience what you feel in a positive, nonattached way. Soon you will realize that you are not defined by your emotions—they are just transient events.

# Aware~Mind

The last of the Aware practices is either a stand-alone package or one to eventually combine with the others.

If you combine them, you start with an awareness of the physical body—breath, followed by lungs and chest, followed by other parts of the body. Then you move to what you're feeling.

Now you move your awareness to your state of mind.

This is different from when you were observing your feelings and emotions. Now you are observing moods or states of mind in the most general sense—a peaceful state, a loving state, a restless state, a pleasurable state, and so on. This is an important consideration in day-to-day life, as whatever state you're experiencing tends to color your view of the world. For example, if you're depressed, everything is going to seem bleak, no matter what.

When you try to resist a mood or mental state, you increase its power. For example, restlessness comes and goes, but the more you try to resist it, the longer it will stay.

The object is simply to be aware that these states are transient, and that they are not necessarily caused by anything "out there"—other people, situations, or circumstances. By identifying and naming the state, you lessen its hold on you.

CenterWidenListen  *Take a couple of minutes to let go of the outside world: to Center, Widen, and Listen to the relaxed sound of your breathing.*

Observe  *Observe the mental state you are experiencing in this one moment.*

*Be mindful of your breathing for a few minutes.*

*Normally it's difficult to notice the shift from one everyday mental state to another as it is happening. But now that your state of mind is relaxed and settled, you'll find it easier to observe these subtle changes.*

*Before you can observe them, it may be necessary to follow the steps as with the previous approach: recognize the state, move it out of the vague mental realm by giving it a name, then just accept it for what it is. If it's a restless or uncomfortable state you're experiencing, place yourself at*

*the very center of restlessness or discomfort, and experience
it to the fullest. Don't seek to avoid, deny, or manipulate it in
any way. Just observe.*

*There will come a moment—which you may or may
not notice—where you'll be observing and experiencing
in equal amounts. Now there is no thought that* I am the
observer *or* I am the experiencer; *there is only the state.
Now you experience the arising and passing, the actual
movement of states, as much as the individual states
themselves. Now you are aware of even more subtle
stages—the point where a restless state becomes a peaceful
state, or the point where there is restlessness and where there
is no restlessness.*

This phase of the Aware practices depends on your having cultivated
a subtlety of awareness that takes some time to achieve. So it's not a
practice you should attempt in the first few months, and even after
that it's a skill that has to be worked at.

## The time for thoughts

You may have thought there would come a time when you'd never
have thoughts intruding on your meditation again. Perhaps if you
went and lived on a mountaintop, where tourists and wild bears
never visited, this might be possible. But in the real world, uninvited
thoughts will always be a part of your meditation. Here's how to
make use of them.

Now that you've observed your broad mental states, we come to
another mental activity that's more familiar.

Your thinking.

In all of the Quiet practices until now, thoughts have been treated as intrusions. They arise out of the blue, they get in the way, they mess with your mental state. And, until now, you did your best to diminish their influence by concentrating on an object, or by filling your mind with physical, emotional, or mental observations. Now we're going to deal with them in a more mindful way.

Instead of experiencing thoughts as an intrinsic part of the "me" experience, you treat them as passing events to be observed dispassionately. As if they were images on the big screen in the movies, and you were in the audience. Movies are made up of a series of still frames that move past a projection gate at such a pace (24 or 25 frames per second) that they produce the illusion of continuous movement. If you blink, or wave your fingers in front of your face as the scene unfolds, you will see through this illusion and be aware of single frames. Life is a bit like that: lots of individual moments that create the illusion of continuity.

Your thoughts are like that, too. They're made up of lots of individual bits of data that link together to create the illusion of continuity.

But in reality, a thought will come and go unless you engage it. If you get involved, it then segues into another thought, then another, then another. A discrete thought about hunger becomes one about recipes becomes one about grocery shopping becomes one about how many hours until work finishes, and so on.

The art of this phase of Aware~Mind is to be aware of any thought that arises, but not to get involved. Not to own it. Or to be entertained by it. Or to respond to it. Just to view it in exactly the same way as you would a movie—in the moment, with fascination. This frame comes, it goes, and is replaced by another. This thought comes, it goes, and is replaced by another.

More remarkable still, if you observe without getting involved, it vanishes without a trace in no time at all.

This is how it works in theory. In practice, you probably will get involved now and then. So it helps to have an anchoring observation that you can bring the awareness back to.

Yes, it's your breathing.

CenterWidenListen *Take a couple of minutes to let go of the outside world: to Center, Widen, and Listen to the relaxed sound of your breathing.*

Observe *Observe any thought that arises, and observe its passing as well.*

*As you sit there being aware of your breathing, sooner or later a thought will intrude. When you become aware of it, instead of returning to your breathing, observe the thought. If it helps, view it as a passing frame on an imaginary movie screen in front of you.*

*Observe how it appears, stays for a while, then passes. Be fascinated by the nature of thought—the rising, the passing—rather than the content. Be in the center of thinking, not of thought.*

*If you slip and you get caught up in a particular idea, just return your attention to your breathing. Stay with your breathing.*

*And, most important, don't go looking for thoughts. They will show up soon enough.*

## The total body-mind picture

You now have an Aware practice based on mental states, and another that is based on thoughts. You can treat them as separate, as a mind package, or as part of a continuum of Aware practices.

At some stage in the future, you may want to combine all of these in a single sitting. In this case you begin at the central life activity—the breathing—and slowly work your way through the body, through the emotions, then through the mind. This would be the most powerful Aware practice of them all.

Of course, there would be no point in attempting this until you've worked through each of the different Aware practices individually.

# The role of Aware

The Aware practices are more than a method of meditation. They are the foundation of a whole-of-life practice that's designed to help you understand the nature of the self, and to savor every instant of your existence.

Whereas the Deep practices do this by taking you to the heart of what is real through transcendence—that is, by attaining a level of insight beyond the world of objects and sensory perceptions—the Aware practices do it in a more linear, systematic way.

By closely observing the innermost workings of your mind, for example, you become progressively more aware of your own true nature. By taking a magnifying glass to your most subtle human behaviors, you learn to be objective about your ups and downs. So you can relate to whatever occurs with clarity and wisdom. So you can learn how to live with the fears and sufferings that affect so many people.

In time you can take it even further and use these skills to explore the nature of consciousness itself.

Key to all of this is training the attention to remain in the present, and to be wholly aware of what is happening moment by moment. This requires a major shift in mental approach. The starting point is to bring full awareness to yourself—your physical body, your mind and emotions, and all aspects of your being. You do this through your daily Aware practice, then by taking that awareness into all aspects of your day.

In the next chapter, we'll explore how you take that awareness into the nonmeditating parts of your life with Ongoing.

There are meditation traditions that use practices such as Aware almost exclusively. While it may take a little longer to build your skills to a comfortable level, the practice can be absorbing enough in its own right to keep you interested.

If you're attracted to this route, I'd recommend that you start with combining it with a concentrative practice such as Deep for the first six months or so: using Deep to train the mind to concentrate, then using Aware to train it to remain in the present.

You could use them as separate practices that can be undertaken on different occasions, or as linked practices where you start with one and move on to the other in the same sitting.

| QUIET PRACTICE 3 | | |
| --- | --- | --- |
| AWARE | Breath | Breathing as the center of awareness |
| | Body | Physical sensations as the center of awareness |
| | Feelings | Feelings as the center of awareness |
| | Mind | Moods, states of mind, then thoughts as the center of awareness |

# QUIET PRACTICE 4:
# ONGOING

Now we come to the second-most-important part of this book. (As you already know, the most important part is turning up—on a daily basis—for your Quiet practice.)

Long-term application of the Quiet practices leads to vast changes in your attitudes, insights, and quality of life. If you were to choose one of the practices described so far and practice it for the next five years or so, you could be peaceful and happy. *Very* peaceful and happy.

Yes, it's true that you might be even happier and even more peaceful if you were living a quiet, contemplative life in a quiet, contemplative environment. They are purpose-built for producing peace and happiness. But odds are that in a few years' time you will still be firmly entrenched in the material world, still working too hard, and still having to face the tensions of the modern age. In that eventuality, you may need something more. That something more is **Ongoing**.

There is no doubt that regular meditation practice will take you much of the way toward your ultimate goal of physical, mental, or spiritual fulfillment. When you look back in a few months' time, you'll see how far you've come.

But now's the time to take what you have learned and apply it to all of your life rather than just a few minutes a day. Now's the time to extend—for the entire day—the insights and deep satisfaction you enjoy in half-hour grabs of practice.

And now that you're familiar with the various Quiet practices, and have been using them for some time, you will find Ongoing the easiest of them all to apply.

# The way it works

Right now, two of the strongest drives in society are to produce more and to consume more. If we could believe what we're told, it is almost our duty as world citizens to do both.

Deep down this produces a conflict. Instead of wanting to produce more, we'd like to take it easier. Instead of wanting to consume or accumulate more, we'd like to simplify. This doesn't apply to everyone at every stage of life, of course, but it's easy to see that the conflict does exist. And that the drives are pulling in opposite directions.

The Ongoing practices are a way of replacing these polarizing drives with something more harmonious. These practices are based on the understanding that there's a moment in life where conflict doesn't exist. Where workloads and time pressures cease to be. Where you operate at peak efficiency, no matter what is going on around you. And where everything you do is meaningful and rewarding.

From a personal sense, this is a moment when you can't experience anxiety, guilt, or regret. But where you can experience peace, love, happiness, and fulfillment. That moment is now.

It's no good trying to think about it, or analyze it, or compare it—you can only do that in retrospect. All you can do is experience it.

By bringing total awareness to all aspects of your day, the Ongoing practices place you right in the center of "now." This enables you to really experience every aspect of life, and to savor every sight, sound, smell, taste, feeling, and thought.

It brings all the attributes and benefits of meditation to your day-to-day world. Amazingly, it doesn't do this in any dreamy or laid-back fashion, but with all the passion and dynamism you would normally bring to your day. Probably more!

The Ongoing practices help you to get much more out of life. Without applying any extra effort, the "business" part of your day now delivers the benefits of meditation: peace, clarity, stability, lightness, and well-being. Without giving it another thought, all your chores and responsibilities have purpose and meaning. Without having to change your attitude in any way, you now find even the most mundane aspects of your day interesting and fulfilling.

It will soon be obvious that these practices are similar in principle to Aware. That is why I've devoted so much of this book to the Aware practices—not only for their role in meditation, but for their importance as the foundation for the Ongoing practices. (If you have a preference for the Directed practices, you'll easily see how these could be woven in here as well.)

To demonstrate how it all applies to the nonmeditating part of your day, we'll look at Ongoing from both narrow and broad perspectives.

# The narrow perspective: specific activities

This is an example of how Ongoing works for a specific activity: in this case, walking. When you understand the principle, you'll see how it applies to other parts of life.

Many traditional schools include a formal walking meditation somewhere in the lineup. But this is not what I'm writing about here. I want to demonstrate how the simple act of walking can be turned into something that's both everyday and meditative in nature.

It begins with the objective of being in the center of walking, and observing it with fascination.

Before you take a step, plan your journey. Nominate a short circuit away from traffic. It could be something as small as a courtyard, or it could be a park. Something that you can make your way around without having to think about where you're headed.

CenterWidenListen *As you stroll, take a couple of minutes to let go of the outside world: to Center, Widen, and Listen to the relaxed sound of your breathing.*

Observe *As you walk, observe each step in its entirety.*

*To begin with, make your walk slow and purposeful.*

*All of the things that you normally take for granted about the act of walking are now subject to your full attention.*

*Start with the physical movement of each leg and foot. Notice the feeling of your foot inside your shoe. Notice the feeling beneath your foot as it touches the path and rolls*

*forward. Now the other foot. Notice the brush of fabric*
*against your thigh as you move your leg forward. Notice the*
*way your arm brushes past your body. Don't concentrate on*
*any of these specifics; just be aware of them as they come*
*and they go.*

*You have no awareness of the destination, or the*
*leaving or the arriving. Only the walking.*

Before you know it, you really will be fascinated by the act of walking—something that you've probably never paused to think about in the whole of your life.

Practice the above steps slowly to begin with, then gradually increase the speed over a few weeks so that you achieve the same result at a faster pace. When you're comfortable with it, you can integrate it into your daily exercise routine. Wouldn't that be a time-saver? Meditating and exercising at the same time.

And don't feel constrained to walking. The same method can apply whether you're swimming, Rollerblading, surfing, dancing, or horseback riding.

This may seem like an alternative to the Quiet practices we've already covered, but it's much more. It's a way you can bring your meditation skills into the rest of your life. Some people manage to do this 24 hours a day. Literally.

In another sense, Ongoing is a way of effortlessly adding to your sitting hours: half an hour of meditation plus half an hour of walking (as described above) doubles your time spent in practice, and accelerates the transformation that only long-term meditators can achieve.

Apply this method to your exercise program, and your daily walk or run produces many of the same benefits as meditation. Be in the center of the running and walking, aware and fascinated by every aspect of it, and you get double the benefits—exercise *and* sitting hours. Physical fitness *and* mental fitness. Peace of mind *and* spiritual clarity.

## The broad perspective: daily life

Just as it was no big deal to extend the Quiet practices from a daily sitting into a daily walk, it's no big deal to extend it from a mindful, in-the-moment exercise into a whole-of-life activity. Exactly the same principles apply.

The essence is to place yourself in the center of everything you do, as you do it, and to observe it with openness and fascination—just as in the Aware practices. In this way, mundane activities become, if not interesting, then certainly fulfilling. Where once you might have considered something like cleaning or filing to be a numbing, maybe even loathsome task, you now begin to see it as an opportunity to practice being in the center of an activity and applying your full attention to it.

When you do this in full awareness, such activities cease to be chores. In fact the only time they can possibly seem that way is *before* you begin the process.

The instant you commence, you see cleaning or filing with freshness and innocence. Instead of being a reluctant participant, you now seize the opportunity to practice being present and mindful. Now instead of looking forward to the completion of the task, you embrace the performance of it. You are in the center of it. Observing it with fascination. You do it as conscientiously and skillfully as you possibly can. You give it your full attention. You are committed to the process.

Then when the cleaning or the filing is complete, you bring your awareness to your next activity. If it's making a cup of tea, you're in the center of making a cup of tea. If it's planning for a meeting in a few hours, you're in the center of planning. If it's taking half an hour off to meditate, you're in the center of meditation.

I urge you to think deeply about this. As simple as this practice is, it has life-transforming potential. Yes, *life-transforming*. Possibly more than any other single approach that exists.

Once you've experienced being in the center of an activity, observing it with freshness and innocence, even the most ordinary aspects of your day come to life. Time and time again I hear people say things like "I never would have thought walking through the front gate could be so interesting" or "I never thought a green salad could taste so beautiful." There is an immediate and unmistakable charm about these discoveries.

It also has a transforming effect on relationships. When you listen in full awareness, you understand things with a clarity you've never enjoyed before. When you speak in full awareness, you cut through in a way you've never managed before. Two people communicating on this level is a wonder to behold.

That's only the beginning. Your satisfaction levels rise at the same time that your stress levels drop. Fear vanishes. You start to see things with startling clarity. Your senses come to life. You see how things change moment to moment, so you have a better understanding of what's important and what's real. You find it easier to let go of the things that hold you back. You may discover spontaneous new understandings starting to emerge—subtle in the beginning, but becoming more revealing over time.

This simple Ongoing practice reveals the richness of being alive in the only moment you will ever get to experience it. This one.

# The most powerful perspective

So far we've covered a dozen or so different practices. The way you condense these and bring them into your day-to-day life when you need to are the two shortcuts we've been using throughout this book: ——≋—— and CenterWidenListen.

By now, the instant replay posture should be charged with peaceful associations for you. And because you've been using the CenterWidenListen steps as the introduction for all Quiet practices, their association should be equally powerful, perhaps more so.

You may be getting the idea that they have an even wider application than what you've seen to date.

Because they're subtle, physical steps, these are easy to work into your daily life. You can employ them in places that would not normally be conducive to meditation, reflection, or even slowing down. Such as on the train, in the workplace, in the supermarket checkout line, in the dentist's waiting room, or while having a stroll in the park.

You can use them to help you through trying situations. Say, for example, you walk into a tension-filled meeting. Under normal circumstances you'd be sharing the tension in no time. But by subtly adopting the instant replay posture, or the CenterWidenListen steps—bringing your attention to the center, widening your peripheral vision, and listening for the sound of your breath—you experience an immediate change in the way you feel.

Such a method allows you to access CenterWidenListen's mind-settling abilities whenever you feel restless, distracted, or unable to concentrate. Just turn your attention to finding that centered feeling in your body, and before you know it your peripheral vision has widened and you are listening for the sound of your breathing.

And because those three steps are quiet and internal, no one will ever notice that you're using them. Take a minute to clear your mind while you're waiting for the elevator to arrive. Take a moment to settle your nerves after you read the Dear John note from your lover. Steal a few minutes of peace and restoration while you're caught in traffic.

You can see how this simple, intuitive process can be put to work in virtually any place at any time. Dozens, perhaps hundreds of times a day.

As these are physical steps, which you've been practicing on a daily basis since you started this book, they should have become second nature by now. There's something intuitive about them. They kind of *feel* like they belong together. You get the *feeling* that one automatically follows the other. You *sense* that when you perform one, it begins to activate the next, then the next. And this is true! After you've been using CenterWidenListen for a time, you discover that you no longer think of them as individual steps, but as one fluid action: like a tennis serve or riding a bike. If it hasn't yet happened this way, it will soon. Then you will realize that you've integrated CenterWidenListen into your life.

Lower the lights, bend the knees, ease yourself onto the chair, automatically think CenterWidenListen . . . and the meditative process has begun. Walk into the room, take the report out of your briefcase, automatically think CenterWidenListen . . . and you're feeling centered, clear-headed, and confident. Say goodbye to Mom, look up at the anesthetist, automatically think CenterWidenListen . . . and your fear diminishes.

There are no limits to the times and places you can use it. Between appointments, whenever you're waiting for something or someone, when you're stuck for an idea, when your mind is full, when you're feeling apprehensive, when you're nervous or afraid, when you have time on your hands.

They all add to your sitting hours. They all add to your pleasure. And they all enhance your peace of mind, your mental stability, and your clarity of thought.

And you didn't have to lift a finger.

| QUIET PRACTICE 4 | | |
|---|---|---|
| ONGOING | Narrow perspective | Bringing full awareness to an activity such as walking |
| | Broad perspective | Bringing full awareness to the whole of your life |

# Which one do you settle on?

When you look at the Quiet practices en masse, it might seem like you have a lot of choices. Please consider exploring them all, one by one, until you have a better idea of which ones strike a chord with you. Even then it's not a time to settle on one approach over another.

The Quiet practices are a lifetime activity. There's no hurry to work through them, as you have all the time in the world.

There's no urgency to build some special skill or prowess; you already have everything you need. There is no particular destination you have to reach, either, or any particular time frame for you to do it in.

No destination, no time frame, and no place you have to go. You're probably there now.

Even before you wonder how this can be, you're already thinking of the answer. It is the *process* of meditation that brings the benefits, not the outcome of any particular practice.

Different traditions will naturally favor one approach over another, and advocates will say their favored approach means something or achieves something that others do not. For example, some schools say that Deep practices are a useful discipline for the development of concentration, but Aware practices are the direct path to wisdom. Countering this, some Raja Yoga schools say that Aware practices are okay for training the awareness to remain in the present, but only Deep can provide a direct experience of Absolute Reality. And some religions say that Deep and Aware practices are okay as ways of quietening the discursive mind, but only Directed practices can provide a direct experience of the divine.

I say whatever practice feels right is right.

Can you see the pattern here? In Book B you'll see how they are all talking about exactly the same thing. You'll see how in the end they all arrive at the same conclusion: that there is no inherent meaning in any of the practices, and that enlightenment and awakening is not a distinct outcome but part of the process. You don't *find* enlightenment and awakening—they are already here. All you have to do is remove the barriers to realizing this fact. Similarly, clarity and stability are not outcomes, they belong to the process. The process alone brings peace of mind. The process alone brings health benefits, and aids your mental and emotional well-being. The process alone makes you happy and content.

So it doesn't matter one iota what Quiet practices you choose. They're all taking you to the same place. Eventually, this will be your realization. You'll find no shortage of people who will contest this view, but the fact is that all meditation approaches, if applied correctly, produce a similar end result. The only difference is how you feel on the way. So let's recap these different ways of feeling.

**The Deep approaches take you beyond the self, to where you sense that the self merges with "the all."**

They produce a sense of inner stillness by developing the skill of concentration. To do this you bypass uninvited thought by focusing your attention on an "object" of some nature. The physiological takeout of this is a calm, perhaps even blissful state of focused awareness.

**The Directed approaches are usually "dual" in nature, in that the self or soul is viewed in relationship with some other entity, and always have a predetermined end point in mind.**

They produce a sense of inner stillness through contemplation. While this is a concentrative approach like Deep, it helps you to bypass uninvited thought by focusing on a stream of thoughts and suggestions. These lead you to a predefined "place," which can in itself produce feelings that range from calm and reverent, to calm and loving, to ecstatic.

**The Aware approaches take you deeply into the nature of life and the self, and gradually reveal their changing nature.**

They produce a sense of inner stillness by training the awareness to remain in the present. By maintaining a clear, nonjudgmental awareness of whatever is happening—as it happens—you develop progressive insights into the workings of the mind. This leads to emotional steadiness, a sense of fascination with all that's going on, and a deep centeredness you can take into your day.

| DEEP | By Numbers | Focusing the attention. Building the skill of concentration. Calm → blissful. |
|---|---|---|
| | Core | |
| | PoV | |
| | Visual | |
| DIRECTED | Formal | Following a stream of thought to take the consciousness to a defined place. Calm → ecstatic. |
| | Loving-kindness | |
| | Point of light | |
| AWARE | Breath | Training the awareness to be present. Impartially observing the flow of life. Centered → stable → fascinated. |
| | Body | |
| | Feelings | |
| | Mind | |
| ONGOING | Narrow perspective | Taking meditation skills into your day. |
| | Broad perspective | Centered → fascinated. |

**The Ongoing approaches take all of sitting meditation into the wider, day-to-day world.**

They produce a sense of inner stillness by training the awareness to remain present in whatever activity you undertake. This places you right in the center of that activity so you perform it to the best of your capabilities, and derive maximum fulfillment from doing so. It leads to a sense of connectedness and satisfaction in all you do.

You probably noticed that each of the above attributes relates to the body–mind or the temporal view of the world. If that is all you're looking for, go ahead and choose the one that appeals.

It's not such a difficult choice. Each of these fulfill the same function: they keep uninvited thoughts to a minimum so your awareness can be filled with something of your own choosing—a meaningless "object," a spiritual concept, a noble sentiment, or the actions and interactions of your own being. In time, this enables you to be in the very center of what you experience, and to observe it without distraction. This leads to a state of inner stillness that can be maintained no matter what you do, or what is going on around you.


## When you struggle

All people are different. Some will read through the practices outlined in previous chapters and immediately find an approach they can use at any time. Their minds won't wander, the activities of the day won't get in their way, and they'll meditate like a monk.

Others will never be able to forget they're part of the "real" world of responsibilities, workloads, illness, worries, and noise. And even if you can manage to escape these most of the time, there will be occasions when they make their presence felt.

Sticking to your Quiet practice at times like this can be more than a challenge. Distraction comes from every direction. Ideas won't stop flowing. You remember all sorts of things you should have forgotten. Your imagination is on fire. The mind is on constant lookout for things you still have to do. You fidget and twitch. Your body won't stay still. How are you meant to sit and meditate when you're feeling like this?

After you've reread the section on natural hindrances (pages 94–98) here are five simple actions that will do the trick:

1. **Create a buffer between events**. If you only have a few minutes to spare, you'll continue to feel squeezed. Allocate time at the beginning and end of your Quiet practice so that you can progressively get yourself into an appropriate frame of mind.

2. **Walk or exercise**. Use Ongoing. Take the time to burn off some physical energy and to get your mind into a more orderly place. After 10, 20, or 30 minutes of this, you're ready to come into the quiet place that you reserve for meditation.

3. **Adopt the instant replay posture** (see page 26). This will remind you, at a subconscious level, what it feels like to be calm and relaxed.

4. **Choose counting**. There are two Quiet practices that involve counting: Deep~By Numbers and Aware~Breath. Use one or both of these. Counting is the bulldozer of meditation practice: it always gets its way.

5. **Keep your eyes slightly open**. Even though it's more restful to practice with your eyes closed, it sometimes helps to keep them slightly open when you're distracted or under pressure. Not only does this ward off tiredness, it quiets the imagination, which tends to have its own agenda at times.

Armed with a simple array of skills like those on page 169, you can enjoy your Quiet practices no matter what is going on in your life.

You can take additional comfort from the fact that regular practice introduces its own stability after a while. When this time arrives you find that you don't have to go through all these steps at all, and that simply making the decision to meditate is all it takes to bring about a more settled frame of mind. Can you imagine how good it will be when you feel this way?

Now, there is only one more thing to remember . . .

## You have all the time in the world

There is only one thing that stands between where you are now and where you want to be.

That's impatience.

It's not your fault that you want things to happen now. After all, the modern world is geared toward the immediate. The emphasis of society is on results. It should not be surprising, then, that more prominence is placed on outcomes than on processes.

But this speedy, result-driven life has failed to deliver the happiness, the stability of emotions, the peace of mind, and the clarity of thought that you now know is possible. These can be attained in other ways. They emerge from the Quiet in leisurely and unpredictable ways.

They emerge when you take a counterintuitive approach to growth and achievement. When you relax and let things happen. When you accept that the answer is not "out there," but "in here." When you realize that there is no place you have to go, no benchmark you have to meet, no thing you have to acquire, nothing you have to accomplish.

All you have to do is let go and be part of the process.

Just be.

And if you really suspend effort, and let go of expectation (as we covered on page 47), and just accept what arises without doubt or analysis, you make a remarkable discovery: that it's only when you stop trying to go somewhere and let go of the search that you ultimately get to where you want to be.

Maybe it will take months or even years of practice before this becomes clear, but you should not be surprised when you discover that you have all you need right now. At this very instant. Nothing needs to be improved upon.

Things are perfect exactly as they are.

A small proportion of readers of this book will already have reached this realization. But if you still have some way to go, that's what Book B is about.

# Before you turn to Book B . . .

No doubt you've already taken a peek and seen that Book B is very different from the one you've been reading. It deals with subtleties and insights that are not accessible to everyday states of mind. However, these are subtleties and insights that are quite familiar to many long-term meditators.

If you're new to meditation, it would be wise to spend a few months on the practices from Book A before moving on. Remember, there's no hurry—no matter what your age, state of health, or sense of desperation, you have all the time in the world.

Everything is unfolding at exactly the pace it is meant to.

## SOMEONE'S GOING TO ASK ME . . .

As you'd expect, there is a never-ending list of questions people have about meditation in general, and the Quiet practices in particular. Rather than taking up another chapter in this book to address these—and keeping you from turning to Book B—I've compiled answers to dozens of common questions on this book's website: www.evenmorequiet.com

This resource will be updated as new questions come to light.

While we're on the topic of questions, I'd like to draw your attention to one that arises more often than others. It's about the nature of your Quiet experience compared with someone else's. (Or what you *think* theirs is.) In other words, it's a question about the degree and tone of your experience. This also is covered in detail on the website.

# FINDING THE QUIET

## BOOK B

# CONTENTS

# A NOTE OF CAUTION

Book B is for experienced meditators—those who've been using the practices from Book A for at least a few months. With any form of meditation, you're dealing with the most subtle aspects of the mind. Although rare, it is possible for some people to have adverse reactions to this.

If at any time you feel uncomfortable with what's happening or feel something isn't right, take a break. Either put it off until another day or consult a qualified teacher.

If you're psychologically under strain, or are receiving treatment or are on medication of some sort, see your therapist first.

If you feel anything might be detrimental to your physical or mental health, just stop. Talk it through with a health professional.

If you have doubts, stay with Book A.

Because if you really want to enjoy the benefits of meditation, and one of the above conditions applies, you'll get most of what you seek from the Ongoing practices in Book A.

# RUSH-HOUR
# ENLIGHTENMENT

Hopefully, you've taken your time getting here, because now you're going to be applying the skills you learned in Book A in a radically different way.

Book B is about the transcendent or spiritual side of meditation. It is not about religion, beliefs or faith, or any God-related stuff. It's about using meditation as a way to spiritual fulfillment—in whatever shape or form you choose. If you think spiritual fulfillment means liberation, awakening, enlightenment, salvation, being with God, or just feeling uplifted, the path to it is explained in the chapters ahead.

This explanation is not going to please everyone. There are some who believe that spiritual fulfillment can only come from having knowledge, following the rules, and participating in approved rituals. And there are those from the "no-pain, no-gain" school who believe that spiritual fulfillment is pretty well incompatible with modern life—which would seem to rule out everyone who has to juggle workloads, relationships, and wall-to-wall responsibilities, or is surrounded by noise and insecurity, or is committed to a career. The subtext of this is that spiritual fulfillment is reserved for those who renounce worldly comforts and pleasures, and dedicate their life to the spiritual path.

Sometime over the next few chapters you'll realize how *everything* can be part of your spiritual path.

It's true that those who live in monasteries and ashrams, and have dedicated their lives to spiritual study and practice, will find it easier. But this is not the only way. Their way is just one worldly choice among millions of worldly choices. Whether you explore the nature of the self on a mountaintop in Tibet, or work 9 to 5 in the city, it's just a choice in how you spend your day. All paths can have a spiritual component and can be as spiritually accommodating as each other, provided that you have the skills.

You already know the Quiet practices in Book A. There are more in the pages ahead. Once you've perfected them, it's just a matter of where you apply them—in the ashram, on a mountaintop, in the workplace, or in a traffic jam.

As before, the important part is that you turn up and apply them.

# From method to fulfillment

Now we're going to take the Quiet practices to another level.

What you've taken from Book A is your way to the worldly benefits: peace of mind, clarity, stability, lightness, and well-being. Enjoy them. But that's only one side of the Quiet practices. The more extraordinary side is what they can do for you spiritually.

The Quiet practices deepen your spiritual experience and

understanding in a way that cannot be equaled by instruction, rituals, or studying. They help you to appreciate that you are more than a body–mind, more than your thoughts. They introduce you to a changed state of consciousness that can lead to a direct encounter with **the Quiet**—the blissful state of pure awareness, the infinite, the Absolute Reality, or whatever spiritual or mystical name you might like to apply. This presents an aspect of reality that is impossible to experience or comprehend in your regular day-to-day state.

Book A pointed you in this direction; Book B takes you there.

If all that seems too far-reaching, and all you were looking for was a way to feel more spiritually aware, you'll be pleased to discover we're talking about the same thing. The difference is the expressions we use. And the degree to which you feel it.

The degree is not always of your choosing. Say you've been practicing regularly for several years; you've found how to tap into the underlying quiet; you're enjoying the health, emotional, and spiritual benefits that flow from it; and you're a nicer, happier, more contented person all around.

Then, *WHAM!*—out of the blue your world is turned upside down. Just for a moment, an unforgettable moment, you feel in touch with something that goes deeper, that's infinitely more profound than you'd have believed was possible. Just for a moment, you're standing at the edge of total understanding and fulfillment. Infused with overwhelming love and gratitude. For a moment you're in the presence of something you can only define as sacred.

Then it's gone.

Confused by the briefness of your encounter, you ask around. Oh, others have had the same experience. In meditation? And it's not uncommon? The beginning of a great personal awakening? A hint of enlightenment perhaps? You mean, this really is something that everyday working people like me can experience? Even while I carry on with life in my usual up and down way? The possibility of such a thing occurring in your Quiet practices is why you should read on. With an open mind.

Before I go getting too mysterious, I want to draw your attention to the Quiet divide again. You will recall there are two components to the Quiet practices: one that relates to the everyday physical world, and one that relates to the spiritual. One is a function of the everyday state of consciousness, and the other is a function of transcendence. One relates to the Quiet practices (the methods, explanations, and physical and mental sensations) that help you attain higher understanding, and the other relates to the higher understanding itself.

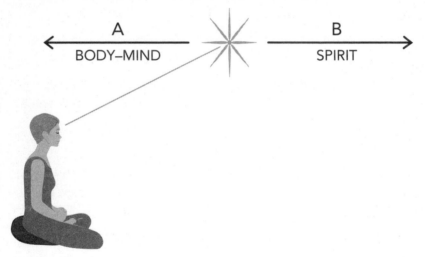

There's an argument that says there should be no need to focus on the spiritual part at all. That if you've practiced without effort, analysis, or expectation, then the spiritual will take care of itself. Given time, this would probably happen. Especially if you were practicing in a controlled environment without the noise and interruptions from the outside world.

Unfortunately most of us live in a world of noise and interruptions. We find it hard to stay on the path—not because we lose interest, but because we lose sight of the path. That's why it's important to be as clear as possible about where you want to head.

However, there are a few obstacles to this. Foremost among these is the way the mind works.

## A deeper kind of understanding

One of the biggest struggles in the Quiet practices is wanting to put some kind of meaning to what happens.

In the beginning, this can be frustrating. The quest for meaning is one of life's most compelling drives. It's an attempt to impose order. "The more I can understand, the more reassured I am that we live in an orderly world." This need surfaces at the earliest age, and becomes increasingly more insistent as your basic needs (food, shelter, sex, love, etc.) have been taken care of. Gradually your thoughts turn to the universal question of "What's it all about?" This causes people to search for God, probe the stars, visit fortune-tellers, seek audiences with spirits, and place more and more reliance on science.

We place enormous importance on finding the meaning in whatever we encounter—be it transcendence, life, earthquake, cancer, or random violence. We believe that once we find the meaning, we can rest easy, knowing that all square pegs have nice square holes to fit into. This works fine if your interest is in road maps, chemistry, or languages. But if you're looking for insight into the big issues of life—the nature of existence, for example—it helps to get meaning into its proper perspective.

The most difficult thing to accept is that it is relative. There is a variety of reasons why meaning is never as concrete as you would like it to be. For a start, it's derived from analyzing past events, rather than what's happening now. Memories and recollections are erratic. Second, any data you use may be biased by what is not taken into account (almost everything), more so than what is.

The next impediment is that most of life is simply unknowable, or beyond human comprehension. You might like to hope that a scientist or formula will come along one day and explain everything, but logic says that it can never happen. This is particularly true when you consider the very small, or the very large. For example, no one has any meaningful overview of what's going on right now in the observable universe. Not from the big-picture perspective, nor from the microscopic. They haven't a clue. There are some tiny speculations and a few theories about big bangs and black holes and things that *might* have happened billions of years ago, but in the main it's guesswork and fantasy. So what hope do you have of finding the meaning in that?

If you're desperate for meaning, look for it on the A side of the Quiet divide, the middle-distance part that relates to the body–mind. However, if your interest is in *understanding* the big questions of life—the universal questions, the "What's it all about?" type questions—look to the B side, the side of transcendence. Here it's possible to understand or know at a deep, intuitive level.

To feel comfortable with this, it may be necessary to look at the way human beings form their understanding of what's going on around them.

At the most basic level, our understanding comes from our physical senses.

Any view of reality here is immediate and raw—it's all about the here and now. It arises from what we can see, hear, feel, taste, and smell.

At the next level, we form our view of reality based on what we can perceive, conceive, rationalize, or imagine. It's all about thought. Everything at this level relates to the past or the future—analyzing what has happened, or imagining what might happen. It never relates to what we are experiencing at this moment.

Both of these levels relate to the body–mind, the A side of the Quiet divide. As they're based on facts, sensory observations, and rational thought, it's relatively easy for us to derive meaning from them.

The mysterious part happens when we reach the level of understanding beyond the body–mind.

This is the transcendent, or the level of spirit. The deepest, most profound understanding is found here. Rather than requiring cleverer mental processes to get here, we do so by *abandoning* them—by suspending thinking, analysis, and sensory perceptions. Now our view of reality is formed by what we're directly experiencing—intuitively—rather than what we can deduce. Unhindered by the movement of thought, we have no perception of time (past or future) and space, but we do understand infinity. We have no perception of shapes and bits and pieces, but we do understand "the whole" (a concept we'll explore later in this chapter). Because we have access to pure, unconditioned awareness.

On a day-to-day basis, though, any understanding we form is limited to the level we're operating on. The toddler develops a view of reality using the senses, but doesn't consider that this might be possible using the mind. The adult develops a view of reality using the rational mind or the senses, but can't imagine that truth resides at an even higher level. The enlightened being accesses all three levels simultaneously. (This merged state is pure consciousness. After many years of Quiet practice you may develop the ability to go beyond transcendence alone, and to access all levels on an ongoing basis.)

You might think reaching the transcendent level would be the preserve of a privileged few. Yet millions of everyday people do this on a daily basis. Sometimes spontaneously—from acts of selflessness, experiencing love, witnessing great art or beauty, praying, or even from suffering or despair—but mostly as the result of activities such as the Quiet practices.

## An understanding for you alone

When you're dealing with the transcendent or spiritual side of your Quiet practice—an experience so subtle it's beyond everyday consciousness—you encounter a state known as **ineffability**. It's where the understanding or experience can't be worked out through reason or logic, and can't be adequately expressed in words or language. This is why nobody can satisfactorily explain a spiritual experience using words and language. And why people struggle to find the meaning in it.

The transcendent level is understood by intuition, not by intellect. You may know with 100 percent certainty that what you're encountering here is the ultimate truth, but when you try to make sense of it in an everyday state of consciousness you flounder. Words and ideas are just not up to the task.

It takes a while to accept it, but you will reach the stage where you appreciate that understanding is more important than meaning. Real understanding goes much deeper than what your senses tell you or what you can imagine. It arrives when you can accept the truth of what you are experiencing. It's as simple as that: when you accept that this is how you *know* it to be. This is called **noesis**.

It is as it is.

I saw a panel discussion on television once. What caught my attention was the facial expressions of the panelists: two had relaxed, peaceful looks (almost smug, I thought), and six were frowning and intense. Why such a contrast? As it turned out, this was a program on religious belief, and the panel consisted of four skeptics and four believers, two of whom were citing personal experience of a higher order. You can probably guess who were the frowners, and who had the relaxed expressions. The four skeptics were struggling to disprove the others' beliefs, two of the believers were defending these, and the two who cited personal experience were sitting quietly as if they had nothing to prove. The contrast in their expressions stays with me.

Rather than any feeling of privilege or specialness, there is an overwhelming sense of spiritual relief that comes from the experience of higher truth or deeper understanding. This is infinitely more enlightening than "meaning," and infinitely more reassuring than faith alone. It shows there is merit in the teachings of the Buddha— who urged his followers not to accept what they read or heard, but to observe and examine for themselves. Faith is good; direct experience is better.

The Quiet practices in Book B are designed to provide this direct experience of the ultimate truth, or as the extraordinary Vietnamese teacher Thich Nhat Hanh described it, "to have a serene encounter with reality." As long as you practice with an attitude of openness and discovery, one day this will happen. Maybe it will just be a glimpse, or maybe it will extend for the rest of your life. But it will happen, and it will be *your* experience. This is far more relevant than what I write, what other people tell you, or what you believe.

You will try to resist it. You're conditioned to value thought, concepts, and mental processes above all else. Every book is written and read at this body–mind level; all education takes place here, as does all scientific, philosophical, and intellectual analysis. Religion is conducted here; faith belongs here; and this is the level of the incarnate Christ, the Hindu avatars, and the Buddhist *bodhisattva*. But there are growing numbers of highly respected voices urging us to explore the level of understanding beyond the body–mind. These people are not just those in the spiritual fields, but leading lights in the sciences and education as well.

But before you can experience this for yourself, you have to leave the security of your familiar way of thinking. Can you stop depending on thoughts and logic for a moment? Can you resist trying to categorize whether something is this or that? Can you stop searching for meaning and just accept that "it is as it is"? Can you continue to just turn up, using your Quiet practices without analysis or expectation? Do so, and sooner or later you'll be enjoying a level of understanding that lies deeper than symbolic thought or concepts. Here you will encounter the infinite—a blissful reality that most of the world doesn't even suspect exists.

This is the ultimate stage of your meditation practice. This is the Quiet.

# Reaching the transcendent

From time to time most people feel the need to rise above the day-to-day world. Whether the motivation is escape, fulfillment, the search for meaning, or to overcome suffering and illusion, everyone experiences this need on occasion. But there's an even deeper need in human nature: the desire to transcend everyday body–mind consciousness, to enter a "higher" realm.

Your everyday level of consciousness is almost entirely self-related. What do *I* think of that? How does this affect *me*? Me, me, me. Transcendence means rising above this blinkered view. So you can see more clearly, and be aware of the self without the usual distortions that ego produces.

There are many ways of doing this, but as you're discovering, the most reliable and predictable is meditation. This involves the process we covered in Book A: your body influences your state of mind, your state of mind influences your state of consciousness, and this reveals the Quiet.

## body → mind → consciousness → the Quiet

The body–mind part is straightforward. Follow a few physical steps—using Deep, Directed, or Aware practices—and you experience a change in mental state that's reasonably easy to detect.

However, when you come to the next stage, consciousness, you arrive at the mind-boggling part of the meditation story.

The starting point is that it is impossible for anyone to fully understand what consciousness is. There are no experts. None. This is a huge realization. Even if you take a really mundane view, here you have the most advanced aspect of evolution, the very essence of being, and we have no way of knowing what it is. There is no shortage of opinions, though.

Broadly speaking, they divide into two camps. The first one is the **function** camp. It says that consciousness is just a function of the brain—end of story.

Let's see if you can accept this at an intuitive level . . .

*Pause from this sentence for a moment, and think about who's looking at this page. Or who's looking through your eyes.*

*Now that you're thinking about this, reflect on who's doing this thinking.*

*Now just pause for a moment again, and take yet another step back from this. Do you have a sense of who's doing the reflecting?*

*As you do this, as you read these words, you will sense the presence of awareness beyond the reader, the thinker, and the reflector. You may sense an awareness beyond the workings of your brain.*

*Where is this coming from? What is its source?*

Deep down you sense there's more than just a bodily organ doing all this, don't you?

If you do, this brings you closer to the second camp. The **entity** camp recognizes consciousness as something that exists in its own right. Most long-term meditators, and virtually everyone who has ever knowingly experienced transcendence, will belong to this school. According to this view, consciousness is the fundamental constituent of the universe, and manifests all that we experience and are familiar with. Even though this is not always easy to grasp intellectually, you begin to understand it when you relax the intellect and open yourself up to the following childlike explanation.

You've seen the animation style where a featureless squiggly line momentarily takes form and becomes a person—doing all those things a person does—then goes back to being a squiggly line. A little while later that same line might become a boat or a dog, but it eventually reverts to being a squiggly line.

So while the person (or the boat or dog) takes form momentarily,

and has a unique identity for a while, it is always part of and always returns to the same squiggly line. One moment a person, the next moment a squiggly line again.

Consciousness is something like this.

Now, imagine that squiggly line is infinite, as consciousness is said to be. It is all that exists. Not the only thing that exists, it is *all* that exists. And while it manifests various forms from time to time—a person here, a dog there, a tree somewhere else, even all of humanity—they're just part of the one infinite squiggle.

That childlike view of consciousness is just one of thousands. They're all somewhat feeble attempts at explaining what cannot be fully explained or comprehended. As you and I are creations of consciousness, we are part of what we're trying to comprehend.

But in nature it's impossible for any part to know the whole. The pebble can never fully know the whole desert. The wave can never fully know the whole ocean. The thumb can never fully know the whole person. In a similar way, the individual can never comprehend consciousness, everything, the infinite, or even the universe—all of which are probably one and the same. It is impossible to comprehend it in terms of itself or by comparing it with anything else.

However, it is possible to know and "understand" consciousness through your own experience. Using the Quiet practices, you can explore its nature from the comfort and security of your own living room. Even more thrilling, your insights will be every bit as vital and meaningful as the Nobel Prize–winning cognitive scientist's.

This is no idle promise; it's a time-proven benefit and function of meditation.

## Crossing the Quiet divide

Your experience and understanding of consciousness will differ according to what side of the Quiet divide you're operating on.

As mentioned, the A side is personal, and is defined by the beliefs and understandings you gain through your senses, your thoughts and reason. Your experience here is linear, logical, and understandable, so you easily find words to describe it. You can even measure it because you've found a way of dividing time and distance into "manageable," understandable parts.

In fact, your view of the world from this side of the divide consists of an infinite number of parts—not just physical things like separate bodies and objects, but conceptual things like mind and body, spiritual and material, us and nature. This plays an important role in everyday survival, where you depend on some sort of separation between red lights and green lights, safe and dangerous, and so on. But it becomes a matter of habit when you subdivide all of life into smaller parts—particles, molecules, microbes, physical objects, mountains, planets, galaxies, universes, etc. And it goes to extremes when you see distinct boundaries between abstracts like good and bad, young and old, healthy and unhealthy, and so on.

This many-separate-parts view of life extends to your perception of consciousness: you start with unconscious, and gradually work your way up the awareness ladder to transcendence. Whether this involves three steps, six steps, or dozens is a matter of intellectual preference.

Unfortunately, consciousness will never make sense to you until you're on the B side.

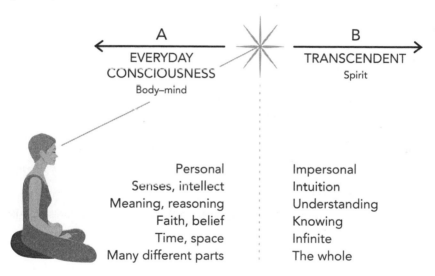

| A | | B |
|---|---|---|
| EVERYDAY CONSCIOUSNESS | | TRANSCENDENT |
| Body–mind | | Spirit |
| Personal | | Impersonal |
| Senses, intellect | | Intuition |
| Meaning, reasoning | | Understanding |
| Faith, belief | | Knowing |
| Time, space | | Infinite |
| Many different parts | | The whole |

Many think of the B side as being mysterious and unknown. Yet everything is brilliantly clear and understandable while you're here. It's only when you try to find words or concepts that explain what you experience that paradoxes emerge.

Your "normal" style of perception does not apply here. Instead of being aware of the separateness of things, you're aware of their unity. Their interconnectedness. The Whole. There are no separate shapes or concepts. You have no sense of time and space; no beginning, middle, or end. You understand infinity. And understanding comes, not from reasoning or analysis, but from intuition, insight, and direct knowing.

You have no perception of consciousness on the B side. You *are* consciousness. An integral part of the consciousness that contains all.

In the first few years of your meditation practice, your experience will be either body–mind or transcendent, A or B. One thing or the other, with a gulf of understanding separating the two. But, eventually, this barrier starts to dissolve. There is no longer such a contrast between the different states of understanding. The subconscious is not so hidden. The dream world and the waking world are not so separate. Meaning and understanding begin to merge, intuitively.

On a day-to-day level, this means you're more aware of what's going on. You see with startling clarity. You have wisdom. Your intuition is alive. You find it easier to make the right decisions. And while you might not necessarily know more *stuff*, you will certainly have fewer doubts.

Some experienced meditators go further. They find they can stretch transcendent moments further and further into their regular sensorimotor world. Frequently they achieve the ultimate feat of a so-called "expanded consciousness": the ongoing experience of pure awareness.

This is where all states are unified. Now there is no unconsciousness and no corresponding consciousness. Just pure, undifferentiated awareness—the Quiet.

# The path to side B

The Deep, Directed, and Aware practices are the predictable routes to transcendence. Follow them across the Quiet divide, and all the fears, imperfections, hurts, and frustrations you once had no longer exist. In their place, you experience a state of blissful, undifferentiated being-ness, and a sense of oneness with all things—the sensation that you're an integral part of the total energy of the universe.

There are many ways of describing this: fullness; emptiness; the experience of the infinite or the Absolute Reality; a dissolution or realization of the self; being in the company of God; tapping into the power, wisdom, and divinity of the universe; and so on. But such descriptions can be misleading, because most people don't "experience" much at all. In any event, they're just words, vainly trying to describe the indescribable.

What's easier to explain is the lead-up to this transition.

Before we explore these subtle stages, let me make it clear that this isn't a checklist of what you should experience. Few meditators would recognize such a neat set of steps, and one does not follow the other. You may become aware of one stage, no stages, or all stages. You may interpret them differently. You may encounter them all simultaneously, or you may be aware of one or another with no apparent difference between them. You may have no interest in attaining some, and some will never be available to you. However, all are attainable for some people some of the time.

Probably the most obvious stage is **loss of self-awareness**. In a practical sense, this occurs when your thoughts and internal chatter slow down, and your awareness opens up to more subtle dimensions. It's no longer a personal experience; it's as if the mind and physical body do not exist. You may sense that you've dissolved into something greater.

## THE QUIET

Feelings of sacredness and awe

Feelings of bliss or blessedness

Insight into what is real

Feelings of unity or oneness

Sense of timelessness

Loss of self-awareness

This is followed by **sense of timelessness**. You'll be unaware of whether all of these stages take place over 10 seconds or 30 minutes. And you feel that you have all the time in the world. There is no spatial awareness, either. Maybe you *are* space.

This may not be such an extreme proposition. Space is generally considered to be a conceptual framework where you can measure things, such as the gap between here and there; or a material framework in which objects can exist, such as the parts of the universe not taken up by planets and other celestial bits and pieces.

However, there's another view more pertinent to this book. This is the view I was writing about in Book A in relation to my boyhood observations in the outback. In this sense, space relates to the absence of all phenomena. The Buddhists call it *shunyata*, commonly translated as "void" or "emptiness"—the field of all existence once foreground phenomena (sensory observations, thoughts and concepts) have been removed or transcended. But it's also a state you reach—one that Hindus and Buddhists call *nirvikalpa samadhi*, or "pure awareness." Or *turyatita*, the blissful state where the observer is one with all they're observing. Whatever name you give it, this empty space or universal energy or "field" is what gives rise to the material world we observe.

Sounds suspiciously like consciousness, doesn't it? So could universal energy be the same as consciousness? Could consciousness be the same as empty space? Since we have no way of knowing what any of them really are—other than that they're all absolutes—space, universal energy, and consciousness may very well be one and the same.

Coming back to the steps to transcendence . . . Once you move on from the dissolution of time and space, everything seems connected in some way. This leads to the **feelings of unity or oneness** that are so often spoken about in meditation—an indescribable sense of connectedness with the natural world, its citizens, animals, mountains, streams, and planets. It is as if, in the words of the medieval Christian mystic Meister Eckhart, "all blades of grass, wood, and stone, all things are One."

Clearly this is a level of awareness that is beyond the rational and the personal. All perception of the self has disappeared, and you are no longer connected with your thoughts or the need for meaning. This often leads to an instant and fundamental **insight into what is real**: a knowing or understanding that is unrelated to meaning.

The floodgates are now open. You're enveloped by **feelings of bliss or blessedness**. Often these are accompanied by **feelings of sacredness and awe**, sometimes described as "divine consciousness." Whether or not you hold any particular spiritual beliefs, you now feel in touch with something that inspires reverence and awe.

This can be interpreted in all sorts of ways, though mostly within your existing spiritual or philosophical fancies: the presence of God, the sacredness of the underlying unity, the ground of being, the presence of something mysterious and awesome. Considering the wide range of possibilities here, it's understandable that people offer vastly different interpretations of it—from an indefinable feeling of lightness, to great lucidity and blinding radiance, to encountering divine forms such as a "being of light" that can actually be seen and communicated with.

Usually it takes years of practice before most people experience the last stage, the direct and ongoing experience of **the Quiet**. This can only be defined by what is no longer present rather than what is. No thoughts, impressions, or observations. Just pure, undifferentiated, unconditioned consciousness. Now you are embraced by silence. A perfect stillness, beyond all stillness. A completely neutral awareness, empty of content.

Some people try to put words to it. This is the blissful state of forgetting or unknowing referred to in *The Cloud of Unknowing*, the medieval tome on Christian mysticism. This is the state of being aware of existence without thinking as described in Patanjali's *Yoga-Sutras*. Or you can just accept it as some traditions describe it—as "that which cannot be named or imagined."

At this level you have no awareness of anything that relates to self or your own existence. Nor do you have awareness of any other. Depending on your spiritual or philosophical leanings, you are one with God, Brahman, the Absolute, or emptiness—but without any awareness of such. Once experienced, this imbues you with a profound certainty that needs no words or explanation, and that never leaves you.

If you look out of the window now you'll see an endless array of people, trees, houses, mountains, valleys. Is there really a mountain there that's separate and independent from the valley? And an ocean that's separate from the shore? And a red wavelength of light that's separate from the green? That is what you see now. But on the transcendent B side, you are aware that everything exists as part of something else. You are intuitively aware that everything is manifested by thoughts and senses. In consciousness. In space.

Take away your thoughts and your sensory perceptions, and no separation exists. Everything reverts to empty space. Or consciousness— the Quiet. An infinite state that contains the whole of reality.

## What if you're already here?

The suggestion of transcending everyday states implies that you have to leave one level of consciousness in order to move up to another.

How would you feel to discover there are no steps and no levels involved?

To explain, I have to take you back to my childhood again, in particular to an early obsession I had with electronics. After I'd worked my way through radios and Morse code sets, I turned my attention to building an electric guitar and amplifier. Toward the end of the amplifier construction, something unexpected happened. An electronic epiphany. One that shapes my view of consciousness to this day.

Most people's view of an amplifier is this: when you want your music louder, you turn the volume control from MIN to MAX, and increase the power. You crank it up.

Isn't that what you think? It seems so obvious—you turn up the volume control, more power is squeezed out of the amplifier, and the music gets louder. Makes perfect sense.

But as you're discovering in Book B, things are not always as they appear. In fact, what happens with an amplifier is the reverse of this. The amplifier is always on MAX. You use the volume control to *decrease* what is ultimately fed to the speakers, not to increase it.

The role of the control is to impede, not to boost. You can twiddle as much as you like, but all you will ever manage to do is reduce what is already there.

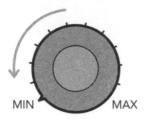

MIN          MAX

Consciousness is like that. The conventional view is that it is some kind of weak signal that has to be expanded or turned up in order to reach "higher" consciousness. But consciousness doesn't need amplifying. Just like the raw power of the amp, it's always on maximum. What makes this difficult for us to observe is the "noise" of our everyday life.

Once you think of it this way, the act of moving from everyday consciousness to the transcendent—moving from the A side of the Quiet divide to the B, or transcending the limitations of day-to-day thinking—merely involves the removal of static. Now, instead of struggling with the idea of changing consciousness, you just work on removing the static: your thoughts, words, and concepts. The very things that consciousness is manifesting.

Put these aside, and there it is: pure consciousness. The Quiet. On MAX. The unchanging consciousness that is, and that has always been. Once you experience it like this, you realize there is no such thing as higher consciousness. There is only consciousness. And impediments to consciousness.

How do you remove these impediments? With practice, of course.

# A framework for the spiritual

If you use the Quiet practices from Book A without effort, analysis, or expectation, your spiritual outlook and awareness will progressively change. The longer you practice, the more pronounced this change becomes.

In almost all cases this will involve an enhancement of spiritual qualities such as compassion, tolerance, and equanimity. For some it will lead to self-realization. Moreover, all of this is possible without any further philosophical input or teaching.

It's possible, but is it likely?

In practice, other factors come into play. Sometimes you get distracted. Other times you get so caught up with the pressures and responsibilities of everyday life that you lose sight of where you're headed. A philosophical framework will help smooth the way and keep your practice on track.

Considering that this book has taken such a broad approach to meditation practice, we have to take into account a mind-numbing range of spiritual and philosophical options. Fortunately, all of the major viewpoints come down to two distinct streams: **Many Parts** or **Whole**. Once you favor one over the other, a raft of other issues immediately starts to fall into place. For example, look how accessible the four best-known philosophical viewpoints become when you consider them from a Many Parts or a Whole perspective.

## Many Parts

While they appear to be at the polar extremes of philosophical thought, the two main representatives of this stream present a view of the world that you can understand from an everyday state of consciousness.

**Materialism** dismisses the views of reality that you experience in deep meditation, and insists that what you see is what you get. According to this viewpoint, truth can be determined only by trusting your senses, using reason, and analyzing the facts. Usually a meditator who starts out with this viewpoint tends to move on after a while.

(As far as this book is concerned, materialism encompasses several other "isms" such as rationalism, physicalism, humanism, atheism, and so on.)

**One God** relies more on faith than it does on reason. It says there is a God who is eternally separate from what He or She has created. Usually this God is knowable, with human-like qualities, and plays an active and ongoing role in the universe. The One God viewpoint is associated with religions like Christianity, Islam, Judaism, and parts of Hinduism, as well as generic God-based spirituality.

## The Whole

The two representatives of this view are often confused with each other because they share a central understanding—that reality is different from how we perceive it in everyday states of consciousness, and is in fact one continuous whole.

**Divine universe** is the belief that everything adds up to the one reality, and this is in some way divine. This is **pantheism**, which essentially means that the universe, nature, and God all amount to the same. That's the starting point. There are dozens of variations. One says that God is everything; another says that everything is God.

One believes in a sacred universe that can be interpreted as God; another believes in the sacredness of a (godless) universe as revealed by science. The latter is known as *scientific pantheism*.

The **non-dual** view agrees with the above, inasmuch as everything is part of the whole, then takes it one step further. It maintains that everything you are aware of is a manifestation of consciousness—not only natural phenomena such as mountains and galaxies, but the sense of the personal self as well—and that reality is the infinite background state that enables these to exist. You might describe this as consciousness, Brahman, universal energy, featureless empty space, or the Quiet.

## Parts or Whole?

Historically the meditative traditions have favored the Whole viewpoint. Not only does it underpin Buddhism, Taoism, and the Vedantic religions, it echoes the transcendent experience of millions of long-term meditators. The Christian mystic, the Buddhist monk, the Sufi mystic, the Hindu *sadhu*, the African shaman, and the Taoist priest all share a similar (though difficult to describe) experience of unity and oneness of spirit.

In the last century or so the non-dual view has also attracted increasing numbers of nonmeditating advocates. Here we have a worldview that contradicts your everyday experiences and perceptions, and makes your head hurt to even think about: why is it gaining in popularity? Why do mystics report virtually the same experience? Why do the evolved thinkers of all religions gravitate to this viewpoint?

Maybe we can blame it on the physicists. More and more of them now focus on the interconnectedness of things rather than their separateness. As more evidence emerges that all parts of the universe are interrelated, they conclude that the perception of separateness is just that—a perception. This understanding was powerfully articulated by the great mystic physicist Albert Einstein:

> *A human being is a part of a whole, called by us "universe,"*
> *a part limited in time and space. He experiences himself,*
> *his thoughts and feelings as something separated from the*
> *rest ... a kind of optical delusion of his consciousness. This*
> *delusion is a kind of prison for us, restricting us to our*
> *personal desires and to affection for a few persons nearest*
> *to us. Our task must be to free ourselves from this prison*
> *by widening our circle of compassion to embrace all living*
> *creatures and the whole of nature in its beauty.*

The fact that I've devoted so many words to the Whole view should not suggest that I'm promoting it. Even though my own meditative experience leaves me in no doubt as to what is the "right" view as far as I'm concerned, all views are valid. In the end it all boils down to preference, conditioning, experience, and what's going on in your life.

For example, if you're hungry or sexually frustrated, or watching a loved one ail, you'll find it hard to entertain any view of the world that does not involve separateness—where one body and personality is totally independent of all others, or where one person's fate or suffering is separate from everyone else's. On the other hand, if all your basic needs are being satisfied and you have the luxury of time for thinking about higher truth, *and you've been practicing for some time*, you will probably start to see the appeal of the Whole.

Similarly, if you have strong roots in a theistic religion, such as Christianity, you'll find it hard to accept any worldview that doesn't allow for a separate soul and God. Whereas if your roots are in one of the Eastern traditions, such as Buddhism, you will feel at home with the view of a unified all.

Many Parts or Whole? Each has a wealth of history to commend it. Each has its supporters and detractors. And as long as they are underpinned by regular practice, both will eventually take you to the same place.

# The three spiritual fundamentals

If you've been meditating for a while, and one of the above frameworks conforms to your view of the world, you're ready to move on.

But if you're still unclear, there's another approach you can take to establishing that spiritual framework.

It's all to do with the fundamentals of spiritual truth.

This might seem like risky territory. There are as many views of spiritual truth as there are people on this planet. These views have led to wars, the slaughter and torture of millions, and billions of words of explanation, as well as centuries of angst, doubt, and guilt. Yet the fundamentals boil down to three simple questions.

- Q1: What is the Absolute Reality?
- Q2: What is the essence of the self?
- Q3: How should I live my life?

As Q3 relates only to the temporal world, I don't intend to get involved in it here. Besides, once you've resolved the first two, the third question tends to answer itself. Or at least it directs you to where you'll find the answer.

# Q1: What is the Absolute Reality?

The spiritual world is awash with hazy expressions like the infinite, Absolute Reality, True Permanent Reality, Supreme Reality, Ultimate Reality, the Ultimate, the Absolute Truth, the Supreme, the Godhead, and so on. There is a range of other expressions that have similar meanings.

In a generic sense, they refer to the underlying truth or principle behind all that exists.

Depending on the interpretation of the individual, there might be a natural or a supernatural explanation of this—it might relate to the natural function of the universe, to a supreme being or creator, to Brahman, to emptiness, or to pure consciousness.

However it is explained it's beyond the understanding of scientists, philosophers, gurus, and all sentient beings, but you kind of know that this principle exists . . . somehow, somewhere.

By definition and logic, Absolute Reality is fixed and constant. So it's exactly the same for Buddhists, Christians, Jews, Muslims, Satanists, and atheists—even if they're not always aware of the fact.

Where the variations come in is when you bring *relative* reality into the mix. This is where the fun starts. In your mind, you are convinced that some things are real and some things not. You know this by what you see, hear, feel, taste, and smell. And by what you can imagine. However, your view is relative. It belongs to the body–mind levels of understanding, and relates to your unique viewpoint.

Because of the limitations of language and the interpretation of spiritual understanding, people tend to arrive at all sorts of different conclusions as to what Absolute Reality is. Committed Christians are convinced it's God. Buddhists are convinced it's emptiness or space or unconditioned consciousness. Hindus are convinced it's Brahman.

Hard-nosed materialists scoff at the possibility of there being an absolute version of reality at all. And many have not the faintest idea.

Generally, though, understanding divides along the lines of the Many Parts or Whole worldviews.

The **Parts** camp says:

- There is no absolute, and reality is only what you can perceive through your senses; or
- Absolute Reality is a knowable, personal God or a supreme being that is eternally separate from the rest of creation.

The **Whole** camp says Absolute Reality is:

- The indivisible universe, which is another name for God;
- The indivisible universe that can be scientifically proven, but that has nothing to do with God;
- The transcendent, unknowable all (Brahman, or everything in existence, or the Godhead); or
- Formless empty space.

Does your practice lead you in the direction of one of these? Deep down, do you sense that one is more "true" or more real than another?

If so, you know where to head.

If not, no worries. Considering that this is one of life's greatest mysteries, it won't matter if you take a few more months to decide. When the time is right, something will arise.

# Q2: What is the essence of the self?

The next part of the spiritual equation is a question we played with earlier. Who is it who's thinking about who's reading this page? What is the source of the "I" thought? Where does the notion of the self originate?

Most people start out believing the self to be a pretty straightforward combination of body and mind, with one part dominating at different stages of life.

When you're a child, you have no doubt that "I" is the body. When you're an adult, you feel certain that it's the mind. For most of us, that's about as far as our observations will go.

But there are turning points in life when you suspect there's more to the story. We've mentioned these pivotal moments before: times of immense upheaval, or of transcendent beauty, or when disaster or illness makes you aware of your own mortality, or when everything falls into place and is perfect, or you experience great reverence or insight. And, most predictably, in your regular Quiet practice.

At times like these you feel that there is more to "I" than just a combination of body, mind, and personality. Suddenly you start entertaining the possibility that you're not just a body–mind package at all, but are infinitely more. Or infinitely less. But what exactly?

When you have firm philosophical or religious views, the answer is defined for you.

A Christian believes she's a spiritual being, a soul with a body–mind. A Buddhist believes the individual self is an illusion, and that he's really "not-self." A committed materialist insists that what you see is all you get. And others take years of meditation practice to work it out.

As with views of Absolute Reality, understandings tend to divide along Many Parts or Whole lines.

The **Parts** camp asserts that "I am separate from the rest of the world," and says:

- Any view of the self is just a simple electrochemical activity of the brain; or
- The self is an independent spiritual entity, or soul.

The **Whole** camp asserts that "I am an integral part of the whole," and says the self is:

- An indivisible part of all that exists, and may be described as energy or consciousness;
- One with everything else—consciousness, perhaps—but with individual qualities; or
- An illusion, and all there is is emptiness.

If you can put aside the intellect for a moment, you often discover that you have an intuitive leaning toward one of the above views. However, if none strikes a chord at this moment, you can move on with your practice without giving it another thought.

Or you can probe deeper.

At the turn of the last century, one of modern times' most influential sages, Bhagavan Sri Ramana Maharshi (not to be confused with the founder of the TM movement), taught a system of self-inquiry that was designed to explore the nature of existence. It begins with the one fact every human can relate to: "I exist."

From that point on, the process is a method of inquiry designed to establish exactly what "I" is. You start by asking the question "Who am I?," then follow the thread back to the source, the origin of what you understand as "I."

When the last thought disappears, this provides the insight into the nature of reality.

As Ramana taught it, self-inquiry was an exhaustive process that might involve months or even years of contemplation. There was never any suggestion that an answer would pop out overnight. This should not dissuade you from using it, though, because even within a single sitting it will help you bypass the obvious, and move into more revealing territory.

We use similar steps to the Directed practices from Book A.

> Before you attempt this exercise, refer back to the Note of Caution at the start of Book B.

Center Widen Listen  *Let go out of the outside world: Center, Widen, and Listen.*

Observe  *Observe where the "I" thought originates.*

*When your attention is concentrated, and you're feeling in the center of your breathing, ask yourself, with a real sense of openness and discovery, "Who am I?"*

*This launches a process, the logic of which goes something like this . . .*

*I begin with the knowledge that I am the source of my own awareness. Everything I'm conscious of—every thought, concept, belief, observation, and inspiration—exists within my awareness. It's impossible for anything in that field of*

*awareness to be "I"—otherwise something else would be the*
*source of* my *awareness. That would be like a camera taking*
*a photograph of itself.*

If you find that too abstract for your mind to grasp right away, you can turn your thought stream to something more tangible.

*All my worldly senses say that "I" must be somewhere within*
*the organism I call "me." This makes sense. Seems logical. But*
*is it the totality of the organism, or part of it?*

Remember, anything you're aware of cannot be "I."

*I'm aware of my physical body, from the soles of my feet to*
*my beating heart, so none of those physical parts can be "I."*
*Besides, I have ownership of this organism, and might even*
*be able to imagine continuing on a spiritual level without it.*
*So "I" must be more than a physical body.*

*I'm also aware of my senses—aware of seeing, hearing,*
*tasting, smelling, and feeling, as well as all the things that I*
*see, hear, taste, smell, and feel. So "I" cannot be my senses.*
*Same with my emotions. Even though they creep up on me*
*from time to time, and seem to have a mind of their own, I*
*am fully aware of them. So "I" cannot be my emotions.*

*The same applies to my personality—which, along with*
*my intellect and physical body, is what makes me who I am*
*(as far as the outside world is concerned). I am aware of my*
*personality, so "I" cannot be my personality.*

*What about my brain? Oops, I said "my." So, clearly this*
*can't be "I." Unless, of course, the possessive is just a trick of*

*language. But if that were the case, what part of the brain houses "I"? No neurologist or brain surgeon can tell me that. In any event, from time to time I am aware of my brain— from conscious as well as unconscious perspectives.*

*This leads to thoughts. Many believe the entire concept of "I" stems from a mental activity called thinking. If this were so, then "I" would be just a thought. But I have dispassionately viewed the rising and passing of my thoughts in the Aware practices. I have also experienced and observed moments of no-thought in my Deep practices. Who was observing? Clearly, "I" can't be my thoughts. (Did I just say* my *thoughts?)*

So we come to the mind.

After excluding everything else to do with the human organism, it's natural to think that the mind must be the source of "I." If you have a materialist view of the world, and have never done any serious meditation practice, you might think this is as far as you want to go. The materialist view is that the nature of mind is thought; therefore no thought, no mind, no "I." But if you just stop for a while and allow yourself to come in contact with your inner stillness, you will intuitively know there's still some way to go. A long way to go.

*Having been using the Aware practices for some time, I now feel comfortable with the claim "I understand the nature and workings of my mind." I am also aware of this from my Deep practices. The moment I experience having no thoughts—such as in deep meditation—I become aware of mind or consciousness. This indicates that there is an "I" even further removed than the mind.*

It's at this point that the different philosophical or spiritual outlooks come into play. Depending on your view of Absolute Reality (if you have one), there are several possible checkout points you may feel comfortable with. However, if you dare to confront the truth, there's still some way to go.

The nonmaterialists among us have reached the conclusion that "I" is not the body–mind. So where is this "I"?

*Perhaps it is the individual soul. After all, the mind is finite, the soul infinite; therefore, simple logic says that the soul must be "I."*

This brings you to a crossroads.

If you believe the soul is eternally separate from the supreme being and other souls, and find comfort and truth in that viewpoint, this is as far as you can go. Better to check out here before you put that view under strain. Move on to the next chapter in a blissful state of soul-consciousness.

But if you're daring, and are open to all possibilities, you might utter the one sentence that can shake you to your very foundations:

*"I have a soul."*

Now you're in deep water. "I" is yet a step beyond the mind, beyond the soul. Where else is there to go?

The more you contemplate this, the more you begin to understand that when the mind relentlessly explores its own nature, after negating all of the above, it arrives at the position that there is no such thing as mind, there is no independent soul, and there is no "I" thought at all. This is the place of pure silence, pure consciousness.

Now you understand the universal self must be the "I"; the self is all, the world, the universe, God and gods. The self is unmediated awareness, which is defined as infinite existence, infinite consciousness, infinite bliss.

Or you could frame it differently. Now you understand that the self is just a manifestation of the one consciousness. "I" is an illusion. This may lead you to conclude that all that exists is empty space.

The moment you arrive at the final step—whatever step that may be—thoughts cease and you are left with nothing but a blissful, undifferentiated state of consciousness.

## Applying the answers

Now that you've been through the above steps, you may have a better idea of at least a couple of the three fundamental spiritual questions listed on page 203.

Remember that the third question—"How should I live my life?"—is something you can explore from within any of the spiritual or ethical traditions. But it's not the business of this book.

If you already have the answers, great. If not, no worries. Just continue with your Quiet practices and let answers come when they come. The journey may turn out to be different, but the destination will always be the same.

In the next chapter I'll show you how the above choices can enhance your practice.

# THE ULTIMATE
# QUIET PRACTICES

Now it's time to put what you've taken from the previous chapters to work.

Remember, the overall purpose of the Quiet practices is to train the mind so that it is subtle enough to have an ongoing connection with the Quiet. Everything flows from this. Your spiritual insight and wisdom grow, the myths and confusions of everyday life dissolve, and you intuitively understand the nature of being.

There are three ways you can go about arriving at this point.

The **neutral** way is when you meditate in a completely unconditioned way. You have no expectation or outcome in mind, and just turn up and practice until the shades lift and you're illuminated. By reducing uninvited thought you bypass the worldly realm of senses, psychology, and concepts, and you open up to a far more revealing realm of understanding. This is how most of the Deep practices work.

The **structured** way is when you employ a specific strategy to remove the barriers to consciousness.

You methodically pick your way through the tricks of the senses, psychology, and concepts so you can observe everything with clarity and objectivity.

This is how the Aware practices work.

> If you haven't yet resolved the two big questions in the previous chapter, stay with the neutral and structured approaches—those practices described in Book A—for the time being.

The **conditioned** way is when you have a fair idea of what Absolute Reality is—at least in a broad, philosophical sense—and then use your practice as a way of fully realizing this. On the surface, this might seem like a departure from the conventional advice. Most traditional schools stress how important it is not to try to condition your practice—just to allow things to happen as they're going to happen.

This is okay in principle, but it's disingenuous. The traditional schools are masters of conditioning. You only have to spend a few days in an ashram or monastery to appreciate how much you are influenced by the ritual, customs, and history. In fact, the practices you learn there are usually so richly conditioned that you experience a sense of anticlimax when you try to reproduce them at home. Even if you learn in a nonmonastic environment, you're still influenced by the teachings and folklore associated with the tradition.

Conditioning adds intensity to your spiritual development.

And once you have a clearer view of what Absolute Reality is, and what the self is, you can add this intensity.

# Intensifying your practice

To intensify your Deep, Directed, or Aware practices, we'll be using an intuitive shortcut that's commonly employed in teaching, training, and psychotherapy. This differs from the traditional spiritual approach, where the process is subtle and circuitous. And where you come at it from many different directions, persevering year after year, until one day the penny drops.

The following approach is a shortcut.

You start with the end point in mind (a rough understanding of what Absolute Reality is), then you surrender to the process and leave it to the subconscious or the intuition to take you there. Whether this becomes a six-month shortcut or a 20-year shortcut, I have no idea. But it is a shortcut.

Does it produce better results than the traditional approaches? Probably not. But are you ever likely to give the lifetime of commitment that the traditional approaches require?

This is how it works . . . Think of your Quiet sitting as having a start point, an end point, and a transition process in between:

- The start point is the self.
- The end point is when the self encounters the Absolute.
- And the process is the Quiet practice.

There is no time line in this, just a transition from one condition of awareness to another. Let's see how a small modification to your Quiet practices does this.

# Infinite Directed

**NOTE: If you have yet to work through the first two big questions on page 203, it may be better to stay with the Directed practices in Book A for the time being.**

I'll start with Directed because it's the easiest way to illustrate how conditioning works. Infinite Directed uses start and end points that relate to a dual, or Many Parts, view of life.

The start point is your view of the essential, spiritual self. What is the spiritual essence of "I"? Let's assume for the moment that you have a conventional One God viewpoint of the self being an immortal soul. The end point is your view of Absolute. Let's say you see this as God or the Supreme.

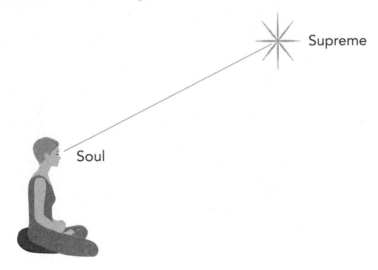

"I am a soul." "God is the Absolute." With those two simple decisions, you've defined the shape of your practice: Infinite Directed is where the soul has a serene encounter with God.

This brings a deep sense of reverence to your sitting.

With no effort at all, you could just sit there—being aware of the start and end points—and enjoy a profound meditation. Just being with God. Very little technique would be necessary, because feelings of reverence produce a similar mental state to deep meditation.

There are many ways you can use these start and end points in your practice. You could, for example, create a visual connection.

If you were to do this in an abstract fashion, you might imagine God as an infinite point of light or energy. A more literal way would be to fix your gaze on a sacred object of some nature. Or, if you were to take a Christian approach, you might visualize the face of Jesus.

Once you've decided on the makeup of these start and end points, you're ready to begin the practice.

**CenterWidenListen** *Let go out of the outside world: Center, Widen, and Listen.*

**Observe** *Observe a stream of thoughts as it leads you (the soul) toward an imaginary point of light, the Supreme.*

*As your attention fills with the sound of your breathing, keep in mind who it is that's meditating.*

*Allow a little time to develop a "soul-consciousness": to be aware of yourself not as a body–mind, but as a soul. When you feel this, gradually direct your attention toward the Supreme.*

*The following is an example of a stream of thoughts that takes you from the start point (soul) to the end point (God).*

*I am soul, a spiritual being.*

*When I turn my attention inward, I'm fully aware of my physical body becoming more relaxed. Yet, as wonderful as it is, this temporal, worldly organism is not me. I am a soul. The body will change, the circumstances of life will change, the world itself will change, but I will continue to be. The soul is constant.*

*When I turn my attention even further inward, I'm fully aware of how my thoughts have slowed, and my mind has become carefree and at peace. Yet as wonderful as the human mind is, it is not me. I am a soul. The mind changes, attitudes change, the universe changes, but I will continue to be. The soul is constant.*

*I am soul, a spiritual being. My nature is peace. And light. I imagine my awareness is concentrated in an infinitesimal point of brilliance or energy somewhere within me.*

*From this point I radiate loving energy outward. Beyond the physical body. Beyond this physical world. Reaching out . . . reaching out . . . toward the Supreme.*

*As I reach further and further . . . beyond this point, beyond this physical body, beyond this physical world . . . I feel I am leaving all the weight of humanity behind me. A blissful sense of freedom and lightness surrounds me. Protects me.*

*I move beyond thought. Beyond feeling. Without any thought, any effort, I radiate love. Warmth. Lightness. Kindness. Blessedness.*

*No longer aware of coming or going, I am content to just be. Carefree, loving, everlasting.*

*Now I realize that I am not just radiating light, I am light. And I am in the presence of light. Sacred light. I am part of the serene, loving radiance of the Supreme. I am forever at home in that divine radiance.*

*Then stay with that realization.*

The above sentiments are based on the familiar metaphor of light. As we explored with Deep~PoV in Book A, this has an imaginary physical dimension—as if you were observing a divine radiance at the end of a long tunnel. Your meditation takes you, metaphorically speaking, through this tunnel to the source. In consciousness, this leads to an encounter with the Supreme.

Of course, you can substitute whatever thought stream you feel comfortable with. For example, if you wanted to add a Christian or Islamic flavor to the above, you simply choose the appropriate start and end points, and modify the script accordingly. All that's important is that you have a clear idea of these two points, you focus on the end point, then allow whatever's going to happen to happen.

All things being equal, your sitting will be infused with reverence and a feeling of blessedness.

## Taking it further still

From a soul–God viewpoint, the above script was cautious and generic. It's possible to take your Directed practice much further. The following example is based on the work of the fourteenth-century Christian theologian and mystic Meister Eckhart.

Before applying this, you may want to consider a subtlety that some people think applies to theistic religions such as Christianity.

It's to do with the unitive experience that most mystics, including Eckhart, experience in deep meditation.

Where the Eastern meditator is comfortable with the concept of the soul being one with the essence of God, some theologians insist that the soul and God are eternally separate entities and that this should be kept in mind.

My view is that all descriptions of transcendent experience are equally imprecise, so the subtlety of this distinction will go unnoticed. But if you want to be more correct, you can ignore the unitive elements and substitute tradition-friendly expressions such as "communion with God" or "mystical marriage with God."

While Meister Eckhart's views are considered unconventional by some, they attract a lot of support and interest today, particularly from those who practice meditation. Citing his transcendent experiences, Eckhart highlighted the unity of soul and God with his famous quote: "The eye with which God sees me is the eye with which I perceive Him."

Eckhart went even further and spoke of a place *beyond* God, an ineffable, unknowable ground of being, or reality, from which all things arise.

The following script is composed of a number of lines and themes from his sermons and writings. It's almost a collage if you like. I've been quite liberal in the editing, the adaptation, and particularly in the substitution of the first person.

So use it in this exploratory spirit and, whatever you do, don't take it as gospel.

There's no need for detailed instructions on how to utilize this. If you've been using the Directed practices until this point, you'll find this is a natural extension.

CenterWidenListen  *Let go out of the outside world: Center,*
*Widen, and Listen.*

Observe  *Participate in the soul's search for the Supreme as*
*you observe a stream of suggestions based on Meister Eckhart's*
*words.*

*Keep in mind Eckhart's description of the soul—as "a*
*divine spark," beyond time, beyond space, beyond thought.*
*As you leave the worldly senses behind, and enter into a*
*sacred stillness, allow this stream of thoughts to take you*
*to the place where the soul finds bliss and perfection in the*
*presence of, or as one with, the Supreme . . .*

*When I turn within I know God in terms of my own being.*
*In going beyond my earthly form, and uniting with*
*formless being, I am transformed by God's infinite nature.*
*Freed from all worldly constraints, I discover peace in the*
*very essence of truth.*
*To be full of things is to be empty of God; to be empty*
*of things is to be full of God. If God poured the whole of his*
*kingdom into my soul, it would be filled with God himself.*
*My soul is easily filled this way, because God is nearer*
*to me than I am to myself. In God it sees itself as divine,*
*containing all in absolute perfection.*
*When the divine light flows into my soul it is as if light*
*blends with light. It takes the soul beyond the worldly senses.*
*It enlightens me.*

*It is the eye of the soul that perceives being, and receives its own being directly from God. But for the soul to be aware of God, it must lose sight of itself. Then the soul sees God in itself.*

*It is in this oneness that God is found. In God, the knower and the known are one. My knowing is one with God's knowing, my understanding is one with God's understanding. The eye through which I see God is the eye through which God sees me. One eye, one sight, one knowledge, one love.*

*The soul knows God outside of time and place, in the space of the eternal "now." The now in which God made man, and the now in which the last man disappears, and the now in which I am, are all the same in God.*

*There exists only this one moment—a now that is eternally new.*

What I find interesting about this approach is that it accommodates a Many Parts view of soul and God, yet also accommodates the unified feelings that arise in deeper levels of meditation. But feel free to vary it as you deem appropriate.

If you persist with it, a meditation of this type can be used to extend your practice until you attain an ongoing state of God–soul consciousness. This enables you to go through your day fully aware of yourself as a soul—being aware of and interacting with other souls rather than body–minds—in God's remembrance. This is a little different from the traditional view of enlightenment covered later in this book, but is a rewarding, perhaps even blissful, equivalent.

(You can find more scripts on this book's reference website, under the menu "FORMAL.")

# Infinite Aware

NOTE: If you have yet to work through the first two big questions on page 203, it may be better to stay with the Aware practices in Book A for the time being.

The Aware practices we covered in Book A are designed to explore whatever's going on in your life, in the instant that it happens, with complete objectivity. In doing this you train your attention to remain in the present, so you can explore the deeper nature of the self.

This is always revealing. When you closely observe everyday aspects of your life—such as your breathing, physical sensations, emotions, the workings of your mind, and your daily activities—two things start to become clear:

- Everything in life is in a state of constant change.
- Things ain't what they seem.

However, you don't notice these until you've trained your attention to notice. If you closely observe your breathing, for example, you get a graphic demonstration of ongoing change—a breath comes and goes, and is replaced by another. You have minimal control over this. When you explore emotions you come to a similar conclusion—an emotion comes and goes, and is replaced by another. Same with mental states, physical sensations, pain and pleasure. None of these exists in any static, material sense; they're just a flow of energy or perceptions.

You understand this intellectually, of course. But it takes a while before your mind is subtle enough to be aware of it at an intuitive level on an ongoing basis. Eventually, though, you recognize that everything is in a state of flux, from your mortal body to the universe itself.

This leads to another discovery. Once you are aware of this ceaseless "flow"—the breath, the emotions, thoughts, the mental states, the aches and pains, the weather, the landscape, the galaxies—you begin to sense the interconnectedness of everything. You intuitively see that the whole of creation is part of this flow. Nothing is permanent. Everything arises, fades, then takes some other form. Temporary form. You are born, you die, you become part of the earth. And if you consider it from a historic perspective, it all happens in the blink of an eye. A subtle wave of energy that took form for a moment, then went back to formlessness.

The more you explore, the more you come to realize that even your perception of the individual self is part of this flow—nothing more than a thought, an idea, or a quirk of consciousness.

You can say this is basic physics, or you can say it's the height of spiritual realization, but it stems from observing the most ordinary aspects of your being.

## An enlightening flow

You keep on observing, observing—without judgment or analysis— and one day you come to grips with this concept of impermanence. Aha! You should not be surprised at this. Impermanence is logical, has some solid scientific backing, and is not too much of an intellectual stretch. But does getting the concept make you enlightened? After all, Buddhists say that enlightenment requires you to realize the three "marks of existence": impermanence, suffering, and not-self. You understand suffering, and now you understand impermanence.

Or do you?

You understand while you're sitting here reading about it, but if you were to walk outside now, you'd go straight back to seeing the fixed and separate nature of things rather than their flow and interconnectedness. It all comes down to your conditioned way of viewing the world, or what some call "habit energy."

Real awakening comes when you transcend this conditioning, and *intuitively* understand. When the flow and interconnectedness are more real to you than the perception of separate existence.

Generally, this kind of understanding takes years to evolve. But sometimes you can hurry it along somewhat by employing a few shock tactics.

You start by challenging the most basic and fundamental of your perceptions—your view of your physical self.

Since childhood you've thought of this as being defined by skin: everything on the inside of your skin is "self," everything on the outside is "other."

That perception belongs to another era, one in which the prevailing view was of a mechanical world of billions of separate parts, all made up of solid matter. Today we see beneath this illusion. For example, we know that when you really explore the essence of a human body, you discover it's not solid matter at all, not even cells or atoms, it's lots of empty space. Some estimates say 99.999 percent empty space. (Many believe the remaining 0.001 percent is also empty space—certainly there's no proof to the contrary.)

Infinite empty space.

This sits comfortably with the Buddhist precept of not-self: the belief that any concept of a separate self is illusory, and that all that exists is empty space or void.

This same view also sees Absolute Reality as empty space.

# The practice

The Aware practices are used to reveal the reality behind the illusion, and one of the greatest illusions is that of the solid body. **Infinite Aware** is designed to direct your awareness to the largest area of your physical body—the vast expanse of empty space that you identify as you—to reveal its underlying lack of materiality.

This poses a bit of a problem. The human mind is designed for contemplating "somethingness." It is incapable of contemplating empty space or emptiness. It's a long story, but it all boils down to the fact that the mind automatically slips in a background. So rather than waste your energy trying to overcome this, we're going to fill the body's empty space with something insubstantial like a glow. As if warm sunlight had flooded into a darkened room and your awareness was bathed in soft light.

The object now is to be aware of the physical self at the sub-cellular level, and to recognize the formlessness beyond it.

Start point = the self

End point = the not-self

So your start point is the self as you know it: the body–mind–personality. The end point is when you see through this illusion.

CenterWidenListen  *Let go out of the outside world: Center, Widen, and Listen.*

Observe  *Observe the empty space that constitutes the "physical" self.*

*Take your time with the following. . . . Be aware of the*
*breath as it comes and goes, expands and contracts,*
*rises and falls. Be aware of any physical sensations that*
*draw themselves to your attention. Observe the rising*
*and passing of thoughts and emotions. Be aware of your*
*mental states as they segue from one into another.*

*After some time of this, slowly turn your attention*
*to the* inside *of your physical body as it expands and*
*contracts in line with your breathing.*

*When it feels right, allow your attention to slowly drift*
*in, becoming progressively more microscopic, going to*
*more and more micro levels. Go past the physical organs,*
*past flesh and arteries, past cells. Then you come to the*
*space between cells, then to empty space itself. Boundless*
*empty space, infused with warm light. This is an extremely*
*subtle state that, initially, drifts in and out of your field of*
*attention. But once you are aware of it, you're filled with*
*an extraordinary lightness. This comes when you realize*
*the body is just empty space. Moreover, this empty space*
*melds into that empty space, until you're facing a vast*
*emptiness.*

*Maintain the awareness of empty space for as long as*
*you can. If your attention strays, go back to observing your*
*breathing. Then, when you're ready, slowly go beyond this*
*to the empty space.*

The more familiar you become with the lack of separateness of the
physical body, and remain in the center of this awareness, the more
you realize that all parts of the organism you call "me" consist of
empty space. This leads you into more refined versions of the above

practice, where you explore the nature of the senses, the mind, and consciousness itself.

After some experience of the subtle nature of observing the "not-physical-self," you may come to the realization that there can be no one observing. Because the optical nerve is empty space, the eardrum is empty space, and even the brain itself is empty space. So if there is any "one" observing, it can only be space . . . space looking into space.

At that point the self falls away, but the observation continues. There is no separate body–mind, but observation continues. Only awareness is present. The first time you notice this can be quite confronting, so be prepared for it. And when it occurs, stay with the observation.

Even when you can grasp the emptiness, and the space looking into space, there's still a long way to go. You reach a point where you finally get the idea of all this empty space stuff. But it's not about getting the idea, because there's no idea to get. It's just about recognizing what is. About letting go of the illusion of separate existence. About realizing that the empty space is all there is.

Even when you intuitively understand this, and can take the understanding away from your sitting, be prepared to spend much more sitting time before the real change sets in.

# Infinite Deep

**NOTE: If you have yet to work through the first two big questions on page 203, it may be better to stay with the Deep practices in Book A for the time being.**

All Quiet practices are designed to take you past what consciousness is experiencing—the things you are aware of—to consciousness itself. Past the content to the background state that enables content to exist.

The principle behind it is simple. You direct your attention toward the "object" of your meditation until the separation between you and the object dissolves. Now, in consciousness, the observer and the observed are as one. Without using one spark of intellectual energy, you are intuitively aware of the unity of all things.

If you've been using the Deep practices for some time, you will have experienced this—even if for only the briefest moment. You focused on the breathing until your awareness was filled with breathing, and only breathing. Then you were just aware. With **Infinite Deep**, you achieve the same, but in a different way.

You go past the sound of breathing to arrive at the background state of no-sound, the underlying quiet. You go past near and distant sounds, past ambient noise, to the background space in which they arise. This is the reverse of your experience in the material world, where you're aware of sounds, but never the space in which they arise; where you're aware of the object in space, but never the space itself. The underlying quiet is the space. More accurately, it is a metaphor for empty space. (All explanations of metaphysical, mystical, or transcendent understandings are metaphors—whether they come from me or any teacher who's ever existed.) Infinite Deep is designed to facilitate this understanding, particularly if you relate to a Whole view of the world.

Let's start with a couple of assumptions . . .

The **start point** is your view of the self.

You believe it's not just the arrangement of flesh and bones that you see in the mirror—a perception manifested by consciousness—but is the spiritual essence of this. And even though the self has individual qualities, it is an integral and indivisible part of the all.

The **end point** is your view of Absolute Reality. You believe all physical reality is underpinned by the one universal essence—call it "consciousness" if you like—which includes not only the manifest but the unmanifest as well.

On the surface, this view of Absolute Reality is the opposite of emptiness, as in Infinite Aware. Here we're considering the all or the whole, whereas before it was emptiness. It's impossible to envisage any of these. The human mind just isn't up to the task. It can't perceive or conceive of a range of absolutes—the all, the whole, space, emptiness, infinite, eternal—that are probably all the same, anyhow. Infinite Deep makes this possible *at an intuitive level*.

Normally when you try to imagine things, you do so from a visual perspective. That's how the imagination works. But you can't visualize consciousness, or everything, or nothing, or space.

However, you can come closer to conceiving of these when you're using your auditory sense. Well, almost. It's a trick of consciousness, but if you rely on hearing alone, you find it easier to be aware of the empty background state in which sounds arise, as well as the sounds themselves. This is what underpins the following practice.

When you read it, it will seem incredibly simple. In practice, it's a real stretch of the mind. The art is to do it without strain or effort. Approach it with curiosity or fascination, and allow whatever happens to happen.

The start point is the spiritual essence that is the self.

The end point is the self as an integral part of the all, which has the quality of consciousness.

Start point = the self
End point = the all

Do this at the quietest hour you can manage. Early morning is usually the best. And if you can do it in a quiet environment such as the countryside, even better.

CenterWidenListen  *Let go out of the outside world: Center, Widen, and Listen.*

Observe *Observe the emptiness (the unmanifest) behind all sound.*

*When you're very relaxed, allow your peripheral hearing to widen. Don't focus on sounds, just let your hearing drift. As well as hearing your breathing, you will begin to hear sounds that are even farther away. Without concentrating on them in any way, maybe you can hear the ticking of the clock and hum of the air conditioner.*

*Pay no particular attention to these sounds. Just allow them to exist in your ever-widening field of hearing. Your breathing in the foreground, the other sounds beyond.*

*After a while, your field starts to widen even more. In the distance is the sound of traffic. A barking dog. Maybe a siren. These discrete sounds are in your field of hearing as they come and go. None claims your attention. None is more noteworthy than the next. You're listening for something even farther afield than these sounds.*

*By now your field of hearing is getting closer to 360 degrees. You're not just aware of sounds coming from the front and side, your listening extends in all directions.*

Now, way off in the distance is something you seldom hear: ambient sound, the intermittent baseline noise that underpins all the individual sounds your hearing is taking in.

Keep listening. Your hearing is extending farther still.

Without paying any particular attention to this, you'll sometimes hear gaps in this ambient noise. It's beyond those gaps that you're focusing. The area of no-sound. Of no-thought. The underlying quiet.

Without applying any meaning or concepts to this you realize that this is all there is. The infinite … the formless all … the Quiet.

And it's not out there anywhere. It's here, now.

You are part of the eternal space that contains all of existence. Not only are you aware of this, you are part of this awareness.

# The thoughtful alternative

We've been using a sound metaphor throughout this book. You may be ready to move beyond this. You may be ready to address the nature of thought itself.

The steps you follow are virtually the same as outlined above, with one important difference: instead of focusing on sounds, you focus on thoughts.

Or the absence of thoughts.

You accept the fact that thoughts will arise, but you do nothing to ignore or circumvent them. Because your focus is not on the thoughts—it's on the infinite expanse of no-thought beyond them.

Thoughts ▬▬ ▬▬ ▬▬ ▬ ▬ ▬

No-thought ▬▬▬▬▬▬▬▬▬▬▬▬▬▬▬▬▬▬

Any thoughts that do arise are nothing more than temporary obstructions. They move through the foreground of your awareness, momentarily obscuring your observation of no-thought, but have no relevance in their own right.

The more you focus on the field of no-thought, the less apparent any thoughts are.

However, as the sitting continues, there comes a time when there is nothing in the foreground at all. Only background exists. Your awareness is filled with no-thought: pure consciousness.

There is no meaning to be gained from this. The experience of infinite consciousness is everything you need. Now you realize that consciousness and being is all there is.

Infinite consciousness, infinite being, which instantly results in infinite bliss.

# In good time

When they appear, these moments of uninterrupted consciousness will be fleeting. You could spend weeks at this practice, and never really be aware of them. Then one day you notice.

When it happens, it may come as a shock. It may rouse you out of your meditation altogether. Then, within an hour, you'll have forgotten what the feeling or impression was at all. You'll remember it in *feeling* terms, but try as you will you just won't be able to recall the experience itself. Then it all comes flooding back the next time it occurs in your practice.

When this begins to happen regularly enough for you not to be distracted by the novelty, you find you can focus your meditation on this state of no-sound or no-thought. You can start with it in mind, gradually working your way toward it, with your attention filled with two things: the sound of breathing and no-sound. Or thought and no-thought. The manifest and the unmanifest. The self and the all. The self and the infinite.

With breathing in the foreground and no-sound in the background, or thought in the foreground and no-thought in the background, or self in the foreground and the infinite in the background, the barriers to consciousness begin to fade.

Could it be the infinite that's observing?

Then breathing drops away. Neither auditory, nor visual, it is beyond the senses. Thought drops away. The separate self drops away. Now there is only background . . . and no-sound . . . and no-thought. Or is it all foreground and all background?

This is pure awareness. This is the Quiet.

Naturally this is not going to happen in the first few weeks. Maybe you have to vary your practice until your mind is subtle enough for it to register. This could happen next week or it may take decades.

When it does, and you reach the point where you think you finally get it, it's a sign that you still have some way to go. Because there is nothing to get.

This is not an intellectual achievement. It is only realization of what has always been. Realize that and things will never seem the same again.

# Infinite Ongoing

It is often taught, and more often forgotten, that meditation really begins when you *leave* the sitting. When you take the clarity and stillness of your practice into your daily life and the wider world. As I've said before, the most important part of meditation is just turning up—putting aside the time and practicing. Techniques, philosophy, and spiritual knowledge are important to a point, but in the end it comes down to consciousness and barriers to consciousness.

When you've made your mind subtle enough to finally see and understand what is, you are on the way. Now you can have an ongoing relationship with reality, however you decide to describe it.

**Infinite Ongoing** is more than a way of filling in the gap between one sitting and the next. It is the way to make the whole of your life your practice. This is why it's known as "the practice of life."

The starting point is the realization you've encountered time after time throughout this book: that there is only one moment in life where everything is perfect and exactly as it should be. That moment is now. That moment will always be now. It will never change. When you understand that intuitively rather than intellectually, your world changes.

The following is not a formal practice as such, so much as a way of going about daily life. If you've been using the Ongoing practices from Book A, you will know what to expect. Here's how to make it an integral part of how you live life.

CenterWidenListen  *By now the process of Center, Widen, and Listen should be fluid and intuitive. Now it may take a minute to let go of the outside world, or it may take seconds.*

Observe  *Observe whatever you are doing in this moment. Participate wholly, but keep observing.*

*When you devote yourself to the present—not analyzing or comparing it—you can effortlessly experience the most beautiful aspects of life: peace, love, compassion, happiness, tolerance, fulfillment, and equanimity. In the same way you can also experience the more challenging events—injury, upset, pain, and so on—with complete objectivity.*

*By bringing total awareness to everything you do, you can be in the very center of this moment all day long. This is the only way to fully experience and keep in perspective every fleeting aspect of life.*

*You begin by accepting what is. Then by using this as your unique opportunity to enrich your practice of life. Everything you do can be approached with a sense of naïveté and discovery. If tea is to be drunk, drink it as if this were the first time you'd ever tasted it. If shirts are be ironed, iron them as if this were the first time you'd experienced this. If love is to be made, cake is to be eaten, overtime is to be done, attend to it as if it were the very first time as well.*

*Then the next time you drink tea, iron shirts, make love, or do overtime, bring that same sense of newness and discovery to it. You'll be amazed at what you discover. You will be in the center of the flow of life. You will be engrossed in even the most mundane activities. You will appreciate everything in a way you would never have believed possible. You will be peaceful and content. (You'll also be more efficient, but that's for another book.)*

There is no end to Ongoing practice. Not only is it a way of life, it's a way of removing the barriers to consciousness.

## EVEN MORE QUIET

For more detail on topics covered in this chapter, go to this book's reference website: www.evenmorequiet.com

# When you want to go further

Even though Book B is a do-it-yourself guide to enlightenment, there is a lot to be said for having a teacher at some stage.

Finding a teacher can be a quest in its own right. Not only are good ones hard to find, they can often be reluctant to take on new students. However, such obstacles may be a necessary step in your journey, so keep an open mind. As clichéd as it is, there's a lot of wisdom in the old Buddhist proverb "When the student is ready, the teacher will appear."

There's no hurry; it will happen when it's meant to happen. Everything is unfolding in the way it is meant to unfold.

# ARE WE ENLIGHTENED YET?

The long-term promise of dedicated meditation practice is an enticing but vague state or event described as **enlightenment**.

Historically, the word is most commonly associated with the non-dual schools of Buddhism and Vedanta; however, the concept of enlightenment relates to most spiritual and religious traditions. There are different expressions—self-realization, God realization, awakening, divine illumination, liberation, or even "finally understanding life's meaning"—but, in the long run, they all amount to the same thing.

What is it? Descriptions vary wildly. Some liken it to an ongoing blissful state, others liken it to being permanently in the company of God, and others liken it to not much more than the removal of worldly illusion. Some describe it as blissful in nature, others describe it as being overtaken by spirit, others see it as self-mastery, and then there are those who describe it as profound relief.

Depending on the tradition or teacher involved, it can be readily understood or beyond human conception, your spiritual duty to pursue or not for this lifetime. Some teachers say it comes from the most subtle shift of perception, others say it may arise from a lifetime of perseverance, and still others say that it only comes from grace or supernatural intervention.

Many meditators think of it as a prize—something that comes from properly applying yourself to your practice, or from following all the steps that are taught in a chosen tradition. Some claim it happened spontaneously in the bathtub or after an alcoholic binge, while others admit that it has yet to occur after half a century of practice and austerity in a Tibetan monastery.

There is a consensus on one thing: despite what the word implies, enlightenment is not an intellectual achievement. While it does mean acquiring new understanding, or being freed from ignorance, no amount of study or research will deliver it. While it is as Immanuel Kant described—that which occurs when you have the courage to form your own view of truth and reality, regardless of what others might think—it defies mental effort. On the contrary, it comes from finally accepting the limitations of the intellect, and going back to your most basic and intuitive understanding of what is.

Just being open to what is.

Because despite all its exotic descriptions, enlightenment is unimaginably basic and innocent. It's as if you've spent your whole life searching for something only to discover it was in your hand all along.

When you take away the hyperbole, it comes down to a single, simple realization. I'll put this into words knowing full well that they will be inadequate. So take what I write, and let your soul or spirit translate or reinterpret it in the appropriate way.

The realization is this . . . *All that exists is the Quiet*. Everything arises from and returns to this.

I choose to call it "the Quiet" because it's a neutral expression. You can substitute any word or words you feel comfortable with— consciousness, God, universe, Absolute Reality, the infinite, the source, the void, emptiness, fullness, energy, universal intelligence. You can dress it up with additional meanings about the self, the individual soul, reincarnation, or whatever you like. You can bend it to fit any of the viewpoints of particular religions, philosophies, or natural observation. But in the end we're all talking about the same thing. The words may be different, but there's no variation in the final realization. Because this is the absolute. The constant. The invariable.

All that exists is the Quiet. Everything arises from and returns to this.

What you are, and all that you perceive and can imagine, is a manifestation of this. All the happiness, peace, sadness, depression, love, and reverence that exists is a manifestation of it as well. Same with logic, reason, meaning, and all aspects of the material universe. Everything you're *unaware* of also comes from the Quiet, only it's *un*manifested. You can't perceive or imagine it, but it is.

This means reality is the opposite of what you currently perceive it to be: not only what can be seen or heard, but the unmanifest as well; not only made up of separate parts, but unitary; and not limited to this lifetime, but infinite. Everything that exists, has existed, or will exist is an expression of the one everlasting, never-changing essence that I call "the Quiet," but that is also known by a host of other names and expressions.

The realization is that you are eternally and inextricably part of this. Before you were born, you were part of it. Before the Big Bang you were part of it. If your physical body gives up the ghost tonight, you are still part of it. Same in 500 years. Same when the Big Bang becomes the Big Crunch and the known universe reverts to zero: you are still part of it.

You can overlay any established spiritual or religious interpretation on this, but the absolute never varies. Only the words and descriptions change. And as we've shown before, when it comes to transcendent understanding, *all* words and descriptions are limited.

Enlightenment has nothing to do with comprehension. It occurs when you recognize that one worldview is more real than the other. When you finally transcend the "me" worldview that seems so irresistible at this moment. When you no longer have to analyze or think about what this entails. When, as far as you're concerned, the absolute is more real than the relative. When you identify with the whole rather than the parts. That's it.

All that exists is the Quiet. Everything arises from and returns to this.

Sooner or later, most long-term meditators are offered a glimpse of this realization.

It starts with a transcendent moment. It's a binary event—one moment nothing, the next moment everything. A timeless moment, so there's no brevity or end to it. It includes everything—the infinite, the eternal, the all. God is in this moment. Whatever meaning you have attributed to the self, the soul, or the not-self is realized here. The wholeness of Brahman is here. The emptiness of *shunyata* is here. Nirvana, Heaven, Paradise, and *nirvikalpa-samadhi* are here. You are infused with total understanding here. In one moment you know all there is to be known, because you are an indivisible part of it.

Yes, it may only be a moment, but you're forever primed to repeat and to extend it. Even though it's beyond the reach of your senses, you sense its presence. Just like the flicker of distant headlights in the endless outback night. *Did you see a light?* You peer into the black. Nothing. *I'm sure I saw something . . .* So you concentrate harder. Still nothing. The more effort you apply, the less likely you are to see anything. But when you look away, you think you see it again.

Same with enlightenment. The harder you look for it, the less likely you are to find it.

One of the most elegant perspectives on this counterintuitive phenomenon comes from the great Zen teacher Dōgen Zenji. The following is my rough translation of his instructions for a long life of satisfying meditation practice:

*Be moderate with what you eat and drink.*
*Sit somewhere quiet.*
*Free yourself from attachments and bring the mind to rest.*
*Think of neither good nor evil; don't judge either right or*
  *wrong.*
*Maintain the flow of mind and consciousness.*
*Let go of all desires, concepts and judgements.*
*And don't give a thought to enlightenment.*

That's the key. Don't give another thought to enlightenment. Don't strain to find it or to know it.

You've been following the single most important instruction in this book: just turning up to meditate. You've been doing it regularly for some time. You've been using one or more of the Quiet practices on a regular basis for months or even years. Without effort and without expectation. You won't remember exactly when the change began, but the practice now comes easily and is an integral part of your life.

Now you know what Book A meant when it promised peace, clarity, stability, lightness, and well-being. These are changes you've seen. When you reread Book B in several months' time, you will know what it meant about training the mind to be subtle. This too will be a change you're aware of. But the biggest surprise that awaits is the realization that, in the grand scheme of things, there is nothing to change. The inner stillness or underlying quiet you were searching for is already here. It has been here all along. Everything you thought you needed in order to become enlightened, you already have. You have had it all along.

When you give up the search and accept that you're already what you are seeking, it may happen. When you give up needing to know and accept that the ultimate truth is unknowable in a worldly sense, you may be getting ready to understand. But for the moment, don't give another thought to enlightenment.

Just turn up, and be open to what is. One day the veil will lift. Something will happen.

It's happening now.